SMART
BUSINESS THINKING
AT HOME

SMART BUSINESS THINKING AT HOME

5 **Life Management Strategies** for Professional Couples and Families to **Grow Together**

Lisa Chin-A-Young
& Mario Bozzo

COPYRIGHT © LISA CHIN-A-YOUNG AND MARIO BOZZO 2013

Lisa Chin-A-Young and Mario Bozzo have asserted their rights under the Copyright, Designs, and Patent Act 1998 to be identified as the authors of this book.

All rights reserved. No part of this publication may be reproduced or transmitted in any form or by any means, electronic or mechanical, including photocopying, recording, or any information storage and retrieval system, without permission in writing from the publisher.

ISBN 978-0-9576967-0-9

Published by: The Marriage Development Company Ltd, London

www.SmartBusinessThinkingAtHome.com

DEDICATION

To our parents and our children:
You have taught us so much about what is
important in life. We thank you and love you.

CONTENTS

CHAPTER ONE
Smart Business Thinking at Home 9

CHAPTER TWO
Working Together to Grow Together 15

CHAPTER THREE
Mind the Gap...Would you recommend
your home management approach? 19

CHAPTER FOUR
Strategy 1- Define Your Home Culture
(Vision, Mission, and Values) 23

CHAPTER FIVE
Strategy 2 - Agree Your 5-year Strategic Plan 41

CHAPTER SIX
Strategy 3 - Memorize Your 3-5 Key Annual Priorities 57

CHAPTER SEVEN
Strategy 4 - Detail Your Annual Operating Plan 65

CHAPTER EIGHT
Strategy 5 - Agree the "What" and "Who" of Decisions 77

CHAPTER NINE
Creating the Virtuous Cycle 93

Chapter One

SMART BUSINESS THINKING AT HOME

THE INSPIRATION AND OUR STORY

THE REACTION MOST people have when they first hear about reapplying business thinking to their home life is one of "hmm - that's interesting - tell me more, what's that all about?" And, most often, once they hear a bit more, something "clicks" in their mind and they wonder why they didn't think of doing something similar sooner. Time and time again, as we refined our approach and tested it out with friends, families, friends-of-friends, workshop participants, and strangers - it is what we have found. It has been the inspiration for this book - to have that "a-ha" moment for more couples and families who then can apply some of the pragmatic, explicit and innovative approaches to managing their life at home and help them to achieve both their dreams as well as smooth the "drains-up" operational day-to-day of life admin and tactical activities that can often either border on the mundane or swing towards becoming overwhelming!

My husband and I started re-applying our business approach to home life early in our relationship. We were in a cafe in Paris and we started doodling on the paper tablecloth while chatting and waiting for our meal. We created a simple chart that separated the year ahead into four quarters (Q1: January to March, Q2: April to June, Q3: July to September and Q4: October to December) and jotted down all the key activities that we had in each of our minds, from visitors and travel to mortgage overpayments and career plans. We discovered that by writing things down and then grouping them into relevant categories to create a single common plan, we could have robust conversations rather than rambling "stream of consciousness" conversations. We were able to focus on items that were important to both of us and, importantly, items that were important to one or other of us but not necessarily on the other one's radar. If it was important enough for one of us, then it made it on the plan and became important to both of us.

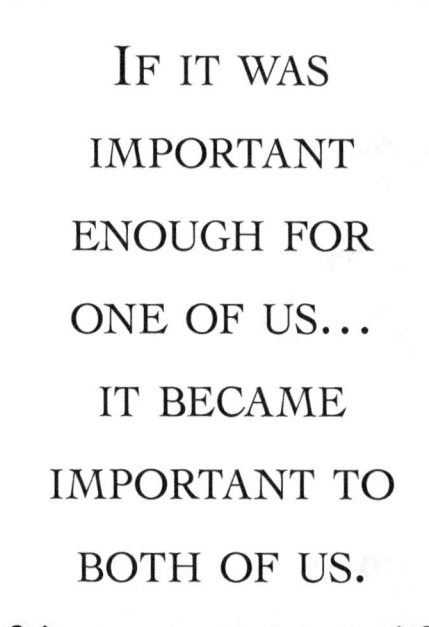

> IF IT WAS IMPORTANT ENOUGH FOR ONE OF US… IT BECAME IMPORTANT TO BOTH OF US.

The reality is that we do have individual priorities and our own "bugbears" that we each think are important and should be addressed. Take, for instance, maintenance activities like changing lightbulbs, minor home repairs, or organizing and thinning out closets with a charity run - these are important to my husband but less so to me. Likewise, things like music classes for the kids or an exciting weekend adventure are things that I value, but that he might not initiate. We found that following a structured approach which gave "air time" for each of us to share our views helped us to communicate, plan and coordinate our activities.

This became the start of our annual planning process. Over time, we have refined and expanded our approach, and have found that in life's twists and turns and the general "busyness" that life becomes it has been a tremendously helpful approach to keep us on the same page and working together in life. It has helped to focus, plan, monitor and to celebrate our accomplishments. It has helped to steer our joint direction and buffer us from a reactive approach to life. And life does have so many competing demands for each of us - work, family, friends, and so many more. Mapping out where we want to get to as a couple and family helps to prioritize where to focus our energy and resources and ensures we are working together as a great team.

And speaking of great teams, so much of what organizations do in the business world is about delivering great results through great teams. Not much different from what we aim to do at home - just on a larger scale. It is actually our background in the corporate world that we have leveraged to create the frameworks we use at home. When you think about it, how well does a business run just by having random conversations in the hallways rather than more structured meetings, strategic away days, explicit plans and constant communication through multiple channels? How often is coordination left to chance rather than clarifying roles for various stakeholders to perform?

Communicating in a dynamic world takes hard work, and businesses have figured this out and recognized that once you get to a certain size, you need frameworks to help facilitate and guide desired behaviors of the organization. Things like mission statements and annual and strategic plans help to explicitly communicate common purpose and goals across the organization. They help to ensure focus on longer term objectives, rather than just the urgent short-term ones. They help to make things explicit rather than assuming that everyone knows what the objective are and what it will take to get there. Coordination across various individuals, teams, and stakeholders is also critical to ensuring that efforts are adding up to something greater than the sum of the parts. How often have you felt (either at work or home) that you are working at cross purposes? One set of actions are actually countering or neutralizing the effect of another - or the "left hand doesn't know what the right hand is doing." Coordination assumes that there is alignment and buy-in from various parties and that your activities have been planned to achieve a common objective. But life (and business as well!) is dynamic, with everyone having different assumptions and preferences for what they want and how they want to get things done - and this is constantly changing. Which is why coordination costs are often high and require effort in ensuring that you are working together on things. Explicit plans, review and change processes, and decision-making frameworks all help to improve coordination across organizations. This is also true at home, where your stakeholders might include yourself, your partner, children, parents, other family members and friends, amongst others.

When we considered the various frameworks and strategies used in the business world, we distilled them down to 5 Life Management Strategies that we and many other professional couples have benefitted from. These 5 Life Management Strategies are:

Strategy 1 - Define Your Home Culture (Vision, Mission and Values)

Strategy 2 - Agree on Your 5-year Strategic Plan

Strategy 3 - Memorize Your 3-5 Key Annual Priorities

Strategy 4 - Detail Your Annual Operating Plan

Strategy 5 - Agree on the "What" and "Who" of Decisions

…AND MEN "GET IT"

An interesting observation in teaching these 5 Life Management Strategies to couples is that men "get it." More than just getting it, they like it. Yes, they like communicating this way! So if you (or your husband) are like some other men that may be somewhat challenged on the communication front, read on: this may be just what you're looking for. Perhaps its down to the very pragmatic and "left-brained" nature of our approach that makes it inviting for many men - it may feel a bit "safer" than open-ended and sometimes "over-emotional" discussions. Also, it's an approach that many professional men are familiar with from their work world, and thus one that they can relate to and even be comfortable with. And finally, because there is an explicit framework attached to each Life Management Strategy, the task is clear and bounded, rather than being too emotional or wishy-washy.

CASE STUDY 1: EDWARD & SARAH

Sarah had signed up for one of our workshops and had been trying to convince her husband of fifteen years to attend with her. They were both bankers, working full time. They had children and were leading a very busy life. The morning of the workshop, it was clear that Edward felt like he was being dragged in. When they each shared what they had hoped to get out of the day, Sarah was full of enthusiasm. "This is going to be the most important strategic day of our marriage," she exclaimed. Meanwhile, Edward's response was quite a bit more subdued. "I'm here to make her happy," he said quite factually as he tapped at his BlackBerry. As they got to work on their first exercise, Edward had pulled a 360 and was fully engaged, commenting that this was actually hard work! By the end of the session, Edward had become a convert: "I used to feel that Sarah would bombard me with various random requests through the week - some were too trivial, so I wouldn't bother get back to her on those as she would figure them out anyways, and some were too big and I didn't have the answer for them. I should have been doing this before - thanks for waking us up to the need and methodology. I like the corporate approach to planning our family time that you've introduced."

At this point, we should say that while men get it, women also do. They generally tend to be the initiators and more open generally to new ways of working and improving their relationships from the outset. We've found that not only women who have worked in the business world, but also those who have not (dancers, Pilates instructors, stay-at-home moms, among others) have understood the principles and benefitted from applying them to home life.

WHAT THIS IS NOT

Well, the other reaction that we sometimes get is that of "So, its like marriage therapy." Well, yes and no. Yes in the sense that it's goal is to improve the relationship between couples. No in the sense that it is much more proactive rather than reactive, and about building foundational strategies and frameworks to help you manage your married and family life. It is more like exercise or vitamins than the open-heart surgery of therapy for marriages in crisis.

Our view is that Smart Business Thinking at Home is something that is smart, proactive, and healthy to grow your relationship - life management strategies for professional couples and their families. The start of what we hope will be a movement in more considered planning of life at home that couples can proudly "wear" as a badge of being smart and responsible in your relationship.

This has led us to an interesting observation about how little proactive training and development happens related to relationships and home life. When we compare this to how normal and accepted it is to have training and development programs, departments and budgets in the workplace, we see there clearly is a gap. At work you can find training for everything from leadership to team building to skills-based training. Participants happily attend them with no stigma attached and with a positive attitude towards improvement and career advancement. Compare this with training and development on the home front: when was the last time you participated in some training related to improving your life at home?

Chapter Two

WORKING TOGETHER TO GROW TOGETHER

WORKING TOGETHER

WHEN WE SAY "working together," we don't mean literally working together as in going into business together - although you may indeed choose to do that. We are referring more broadly to doing things together with a joint purpose. As with any great team, it is so important to share common goals and be working alongside each other, synergistically and constructively, to achieve these goals.

For many, raising a family is one of the key "projects" that couples do together and sometimes the glue that binds them together. We believe that making our many joint projects explicit - some may be big ones like raising a family or looking after elderly parents or relocating to a new country, but there are many smaller projects in our lives that also need our attention. Some of these might be more important for one of you than the other. It is important that there is a process to understand what these are and to approach them as a joint team.

Too often we find that our lives get so busy that we realize we haven't been navigating through our lives together. Perhaps, it's a stay-at-home mom or dad and a breadwinner spouse who end up leading parallel lives, as their day-to-day realities are so different and it becomes hard to relate to each other. Or perhaps it's the dual-career family where both partners are so caught up in work that they have little energy left over for their home life. Or perhaps it is the couple who focused on raising their kids, but realized that, over time, they grew apart as they had little more than the kids in common.

Any good team needs to refresh its purpose and re-clarify its common goals as time goes on to motivate and re-focus the group. This helps the team to work synergistically together, rather than at cross-purposes. It's no different at home, and this typically doesn't happen robustly through osmosis or chance alone. Ensuring that you both know what you are working on together will help you meet those goals and enjoy both the journey of having achieved it together as well as the final destination. It will also mean that when things don't go as planned, you are on the same page and are less likely to blame each other or have misunderstandings over it.

Growing Together

So when we started thinking about what the end benefit or aim from our married life was, we had to conclude that for us it was to grow together over the years. Clearly, along the way we want to achieve various things together like raising wonderful children, enjoying relationships with family and friends, contributing to others and the causes we support, earning enough to support our desired lifestyle, etc. But at the end of the day, when we are both quite old and in our rocking chairs, we would like to be able to claim that through

> "Marriage is about doubling your joys and halving your burdens."

our years and journeys together have we grown together. We would like to feel that we were closer after all our years together than we were on the day that we were married.

And to grow together, we realize that many things need to fall into place, but most of all we need to work together to get there. This includes making sure we are communicating and supporting and celebrating our journey every day.

Perhaps because we met relatively late in life after establishing our respective careers, we appreciate having found each other. In some ways, finding each other was harder than establishing our careers, and as such, we don't take that for granted and want to work hard and smart together to grow together every year.

One of the sayings that resonated with us as an engaged couple and has remained a belief through our married life is that:

"Marriage is about doubling your joys and halving your burdens."

49% CLAIM TO GROW TOGETHER

In research placed amongst married individuals in London[1], we found that only 49% claimed that they had "definitely grown together." About another quarter claimed they had "somewhat grown together," and the final quarter either felt they "stayed about the same," had "somewhat grown apart," or had "definitely grown apart."

---

[1] Based on Research placed by The Marriage Development Company 2011. Online survey of 150 married individuals (50% Female, 50% male) aged 30 and 50 years old, living in Greater London and university educated.

Our Research:
Only 49% have "Definitely grown together"

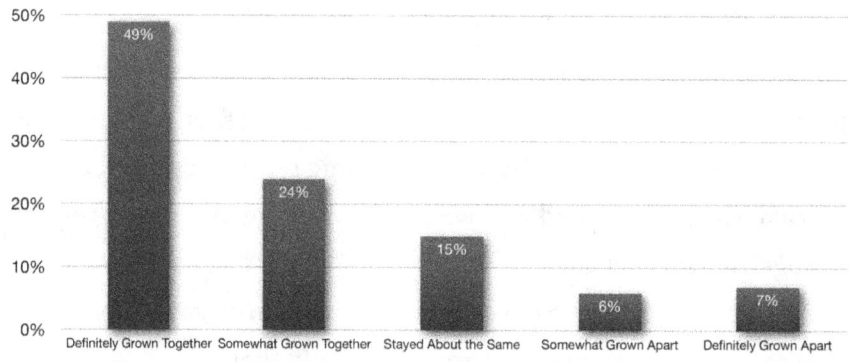

How would you respond? Do you feel that, over time, you have grown together in your relationship?

Chapter Three

MIND THE GAP... WOULD YOU RECOMMEND YOUR APPROACH?

TRUE TO OUR roots in the business world, as we embarked on the project of deciding whether there was a customer need for our 5 Life Management Strategies, we included in our research a key customer satisfaction question. Many of you may have come across this relatively standard survey question: "How likely are you to recommend (whichever product or service is being surveyed) to a family or friend?" be it banking or a type of car or a cereal. It is a common survey question used to measure advocacy, which is a metric linked to loyalty and satisfaction. So, we thought it would be interesting to see what people thought of their approach to marriage and whether they might recommend their ways of working to friends or family.

The question we surveyed[2] was:

"Overall, how likely are you to recommend the way you and your spouse communicate, plan, and make joint decisions as an effective model for a friend or colleague to follow?"

---

[2] Based on Research placed by The Marriage Development Company 2011.

Now, before we share the results, we should say that the standard methodology is to measure results on a scale of 0-10 with 0 being "not at all likely" and 10 being "extremely likely." Respondents answering 9-10 are then considered to be "advocates" - in other words, proponents - and likely to spread positive word-of-mouth, while those rating 0-6 are considered "detractors" who may spread negative word-of-mouth. Those rating 7-8 are considered "passives," who will neither spread positive nor negative word-of-mouth.

> How likely are you to recommend the way you and your spouse communicate, plan and make joint decisions…?

Clearly, the desire for the product or service being measured is to achieve a greater proportion of advocates and a lower proportion of detractors. The score used to indicate this is called the "Net Promoter Score[3]," which is calculated by taking the proportion of advocates less the proportion of detractors. A higher score indicates higher loyalty.

Now, while it may be a little innovative to apply this as an approach to measuring marriage, we feel that it is indicative and insightful as to the overall satisfaction level. This measure has been applied to various other sectors and not limited to paid-for services or products - including areas like measuring patient satisfaction of public healthcare providers.

The results were interesting. 25% of respondents were "advocates,"

---

[3] Net Promoter Score is a customer loyalty metric developed by (and a registered trademark of) Fred Reichheld, Bain & Company, and Satmetrix.

(scoring 9-10) while 45% were "detractors," (scoring 0-6) with the remaining 30% being "passives" (scoring 7-8). So only 25% of respondents are likely to be spreading positive word-of-mouth on the way they communicate, plan, and make joint decisions, while 45% are likely to be dissatisfied and spreading negative word- of-mouth. Perhaps that's why we tend to hear more griping and complaining than positive tips being shared amongst friends!

We were also curious to see how this compared to other products and industries as a benchmark. So we calculated the Net Promoter Score for our survey question by taking the 25% advocates less the 45% detractors and ended up with a Net Promoter Score of -20%. For perspective, by comparing this to 2011 European Benchmarks from Satmetrix, we can see that it trails the likes of Apple at +69% and the banking industry average of 0. But is ahead of the utilities average of -34%[4]... so not exactly in the upper range of satisfaction!

Our Research : Net Promoter Score

Q. Overall, how likely are you to recommend the way you and your spouse communicate, plan, and make joint decisions as an effective model for a friend or colleague to follow?
(On a scale of 0 to 10 - select one)

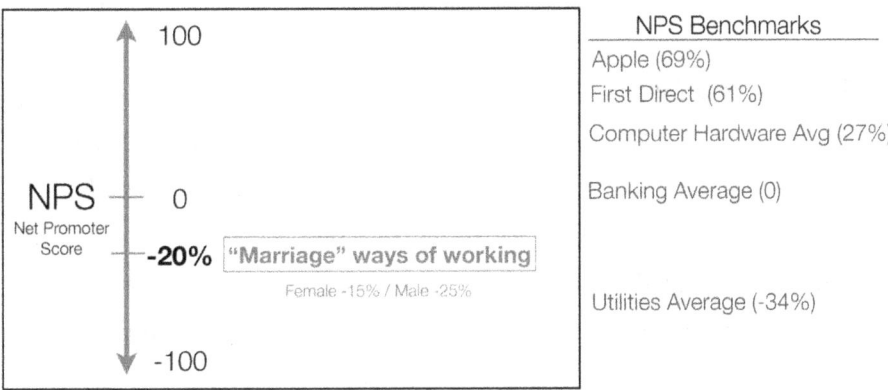

Sources: 1. The Marriage Development Company Research August 2011, 2. Net Promoter benchmarks Europe 2011 www.netpromoter.com/resources/article25.jsp
© 2011-2013 Copyright The Marriage Development Company Ltd. All rights reserved.   www.TheMarriageDevelopmentCompany.com

---

[4] Net Promoter Benchmarks Europe 2011 research conducted by Satmetrix.

Based on this, we concluded that there was definitely room for improvement.

If so many couples weren't convinced that their approach was good enough to recommend to their friends and family, were they doing enough to improve it?

Perhaps one of the issues is one of expectations with passives settling for things being okay … not great, but good enough. Clearly, everyone's situation is unique, but how do we create a movement where we aim a bit higher in our personal life to go from the cliché "good" to "great"?

How do we get stronger foundational skills and a better toolkit for communicating and coordinating at home? This takes us back to the analogy of getting more exercise and vitamins rather than waiting for the onset of a crisis. How many of those detractors who were clearly dissatisfied with their ways of working had attempted to get some help or learn other ways of working early enough on? It seems that at times one party might be more receptive to getting help, and the other perhaps more resistant. How do we reposition getting help from its common status as a stigma to more of a continual learning process that is a badge of being smart and responsible in a marriage? And thus becoming more analogous to career development in the workplace where training in the form of leadership, team building, people skills or technical skills is the accepted norm.

So when it comes to the way you and your spouse communicate, plan and make joint decisions, are you an advocate, detractor or passive?

The next chapters will introduce The 5 Life Management Strategies that couples have found to be innovative, revolutionary, pragmatic and insightful in their lives. We will introduce each of these strategies in their business context and, importantly, will demonstrate how to reapply them to home life. We hope that you also will enjoy applying them to work together and grow together in your journey of life.

Chapter Four

STRATEGY 1: DEFINE YOUR HOME CULTURE (VISION, MISSION, VALUES)

Culture: something that means so much and defines so much of who we are and how we behave. Whether it is culture from a country and heritage perspective or culture from a corporate perspective, it is a lens through which certain actions or behaviors may seem acceptable or not, appropriate or not. It is something that influences so much, but is often hard to define or put your finger on, as it is most visible as the output rather than the inputs. For those of you who have travelled or have had the benefit of being exposed to various national cultures, you will relate to this.

Take, for example, sushi. While sushi and eating raw fish is quite an accepted food in many places now, a few decades ago it was not very widespread outside of Japan. Some may still find eating raw fish not to their taste, as it was not culturally practiced or accepted when they grew up. Another example is horse meat. I spent a year in France at business school and I was very surprised when I came across horse meat steaks in the refrigerated section of my local Carrefour supermarket. But clearly, if they were selling it, someone was buying it and consuming it! Finally, it also surprised me to see dog meat restaurants in South Korea when I was there for the 2002 World Cup. Clearly, in each case, it is normal to their respective cultures, but perhaps not so normal to mine.

Let's look at another example of cultural behaviors - time management. Those of you who are familiar with Latin American culture will know that meetings or social engagements always start after the stated time. Contrast this with British time management, where your invitation will usually state something like "6:30 for 7:00pm"; in other words, get there at 6:30 for a prompt 7pm start! In contrast, if you receive an invitation for a 7pm start in Latin America, you may very well still be the first person there if you show up at 8pm!

So, why is horse meat normal in France and why does 7pm actually mean 8pm or later in Latin America? Culture clearly plays a role.

Similarly, when we look at cultures within organizations and companies, these can and do differ dramatically. Sometimes, corporate cultures take on the personality of their leaders and sometimes the corporate cultures are so strong and entrenched that they have longevity beyond any given leader.

Why is it that in some departments or companies working until 7 or 8pm is the norm, while in other staying past 5pm is rare?

Why is it that some companies will readily invest in staff development programs or social initiatives while others wouldn't dream of doing so?

Why is it that some companies may have a "grey zone" for moral or ethical decisions while others may see the same issues as clearly as black and white?

Why is it that some companies are ruled by top-down management while others empower staff and foster an entrepreneurial spirit?

Culture plays a role in all of the above. Culture is also a difficult thing to shift as everyone in the organization plays a role in defining it through their actions. So cultures change slowly as behaviors change, but they will only change if the change in actions is consistent, which sometimes makes it tricky when there are various stakeholders involved. It can be catalyzed by a concerted and explicit desire to move towards a new culture. Often, this may be as a result of dissatisfaction from employees (for example, staff retention issues) or perhaps customer dissatisfaction (for example, a corporate culture that is internally vs. externally focused) or undesirable behaviors (for example, excessive risk-taking in the banking culture).

Joint ventures (JVs) or acquisitions, where two companies form alliances or merge, are also business "marriages" where culture often plays a critical role in the success or failure of the new merged entity. Culture is often cited as the reason why some of these mergers fail - where the ways of working are so inconsistent that it is not possible to gain synergies from them working together.

New ventures also often take the time to define the culture they want (for example, the more relaxed and casual culture of many Silicon valley start-ups versus the more traditional rules-based corporate culture). Take the example of Google, who states as one of their beliefs: "You can be serious without a suit."

And, so too, we believe that there is a benefit in explicitly defining your desired culture at home. Let's face it: no matter how similar we are to our partner, we are different individuals with different upbringings that have shaped our views on life. There are going to be things that we disagree on or do differently. The classic ones that come up are approaches in raising kids or approaches to spending or saving money. By having the conversation up front on culture, you can anticipate and work through differences at the planning stage rather than in the heat-of-the-moment disagreements.

It also sets the stage for taking a big picture look at your home life - your individual goals, your relationship and your family and friends. This is why defining your home culture is the first of our Life Management Strategies. It will guide your behaviors and acknowledge your goals, but will require consistency in execution to do so, and thus alignment between you and your partner is important. It will define what your children view as normal or acceptable and will be a model for their behaviors going forward.

How do we define our home culture?

Three statements that are often used to help define and make culture explicit are a vision statement, a mission statement, and a values statement. Each of these is used to describe a slightly different element of culture.

Vision: A statement of where you want to be in the future

Mission: A statement of purpose – typically includes a goal and clarifies where to spend your energy (e.g., who we are and what we do)

Values: Beliefs or principles that will guide decision-making

Vision, mission, and values statements help to:

- Clarify
- Focus Energy
- Motivate
- Guide Decision Making

Those of you who have been involved in exercises in the workplace or other organizations in defining vision, mission, and values will know that it is not an exact science, but rather an iterative process across the organization of coming to a limited set of words that best captures the desired sentiment of each. It is as much a listening and engagement exercise as it is a visioning and leadership one. At the end of the day, unless stakeholders buy into the vision, mission, and/or values statements, their behaviors will not reflect them and the culture will not come "alive" in practice. In short, it is much more than a paper exercise, but the paper exercise is important in the process of being explicit, choiceful and providing a clear and consistent focus.

So, before we start, you'll need to have an idea of what your joint future goals look like. The reality is that life is busy, and there are so many demands that are coming our way (work, kids, parents, friends, you name it) that many of us are living our lives tactically and reactively on a day-to-day basis. We rarely, if ever, take the time to step back together, consider our joint big picture and ensure that we are pointing our navigational compass in the right direction. Strategy, by its nature, looks at the mid to long-term time horizon. It is an exercise that encourages us to fast-forward to future states and make choices about where we want to be. By defining these future states, we can then look back at where we are and the choices we need to make to get there. We will examine this in more detail as we review Life Management Strategy 2, but for the purposes of defining your home culture, you will need a common view of your desired goals at various life stages. This will help to then define the type of culture that will help you get there.

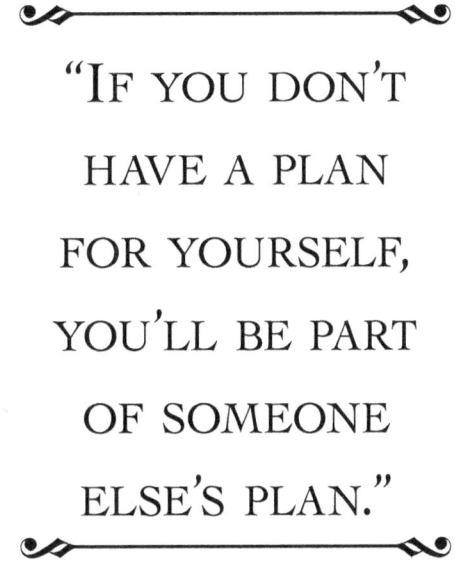

"IF YOU DON'T HAVE A PLAN FOR YOURSELF, YOU'LL BE PART OF SOMEONE ELSE'S PLAN."

One saying which we feel captures this sentiment well is:

"If you don't have a plan for yourself, you'll be part of someone else's plan."

We feel that this captures the essence of why it is important to take the time to clarify what you want out of your joint life. In the absence of this clarity, you may simply drift along with others' plans for you (including your work's plans!) which may or may not be what you would otherwise choose for your lives.

Creating Your 360 Vision Worksheet™

We call this comprehensive review of your long-term goals a "360 Vision Worksheet™". Filling this out is incredibly insightful, and completing it together with your spouse will most certainly enable important conversations that you may not yet have had. The premise behind the exercise is that most of us have preconceived ideas of what we want to be doing at different life stages with various different elements of our lives and/or things that we would like to do with our loved ones at their various life stages (for example, while our parents are in healthy retirement or when our kids are teenagers). However, we rarely, if ever, actually put all of these goals down on paper in a structured way. And then, to layer on top of this various life categories such as career, personal development, property, travel, etc. and consider each of these explicitly almost never happens. And finally, to do this alongside our partner considering their various goals and their impact on ours is almost unheard of. The wealth of information and input for consideration that it yields is tremendous. It is a terrific communication and alignment framework for long-term planning and a foundational basis for defining your home culture through your vision, mission, and values statements.

Let's take this one step at a time.

Step 1: 360 Vision Worksheet™:
Set up the key relationships in your life stages framework

Make a chart similar to the one below where you take the current year ("Today") and add on increments of 5, 10, 20 and 30 years to today's year in each of the next columns. Then, in each of the 4 rows, under your "Today" column, add:

1. Your/your spouse's current age
2. Each of your children's current ages
3. Your parents' ages, if applicable

4. Anyone else's age that is central to your life and may in some way be dependent on you, if applicable (for example, an elderly single aunt)

		Today (2013)	+5 Years (2018)	+10 Years (2023)	+ 20 Years (2033)	+30 Years (2043)
Age Benchmarks:	Self/Spouse	35/40				
	Kids	1/5				
	Parents	65/70				
	Other					

Step 1 - 360 Vision Worksheet™

STEP 2: 360 VISION WORKSHEET™:
Do the life stage age "math"

For each of the above key relationships, now add on the years (+5, +10, +20, +30) under the respective columns.

For example, if your/your spouse's age is 35/40 today (2013), then under the +5 years column (2018), you would enter 40/45; under the +10 years (2023) column, you would enter 45/50, and so on.

Continue doing this for your children, parents and any other key relationships you would like to consider.

		Today (2013)	+5 Years (2018)	+10 Years (2023)	+ 20 Years (2033)	+30 Years (2043)
Age Benchmarks:	Self/Spouse	35/40	40/45	45/50	55/60	65/70
	Kids	1/5	6/10	11/15	21/25	31/35
	Parents	65/70	70/75	75/80	85/90	95/100
	Other					

Step 2 - 360 Vision Worksheet™

STEP 3: 360 VISION WORKSHEET™:
Choose your categories for your goal evaluation

The idea here is to include categories that reflect a 360-degree view of the key areas of your life. Not at a detailed level, but at a high level. We have found that the ones below generally work for most couples and families:

Self, Spouse, Family, Career, Health, Personal Development, Finance & Property, Travel & Visitors, Entertainment, Spiritual Growth.

These become the rows of your table, for which you will consider any relevant goals through your/your loved ones' life stages. Add any other categories that you consider to be important in a chart that will look something like the one below.

		Today (2013)	+5 Years (2018)	+10 Years (2023)	+ 20 Years (2033)	+30 Years (2043)
Age Benchmarks:	Self/Spouse	35/40	40/45	45/50	55/60	65/70
	Kids	1/5	6/10	11/15	21/25	31/35
	Parents	65/70	70/75	75/80	85/90	95/100
	Other					
	Spouse 1					
	Spouse 2					
	Family					
	Health					
	etc					

Step 3 - 360 Vision Worksheet™

STEP 4: 360 VISION WORKSHEET™:
Fast forwarding and recording your goals

Now that you have the framework, life stages and key categories completed, Step 4 has you project forward and start to record the goals for different categories explicitly. For example, recognizing how much quality time you have with your aging parents and what you would like to do with them before they are seventy or eighty. Or perhaps identifying that it is important for you to complete a marathon before you are fifty. Or that you'd like to travel to Australia with your kids before they are eighteen. Or that you'd like to have your mortgage paid off by the time you are forty-five.

Completing the 360 Vision Worksheet™ helps you to gain the helicopter view of goals that are important for you and your spouse over a long-term view of your life by tapping into expectations that you may have for different life stages. By identifying and recording this information into bite-sized bits that are easy for you and your spouse to digest, it facilitates conversation and communication about them. You may have very similar and synergistic goals, or perhaps very different and contrasting ones, or even individual goals that will require your spouse's support. Whatever the case, you now have a common view of these goals from which you can work through any areas of contention (for example, you might not be able to both accelerate your mortgage payments and fulfill all your travel desires concurrently).

One thing to note is that there is no need to fill out every box in your table; the idea is to fill out the ones most relevant to you. For example, if you know you want to complete a marathon by the time you are fifty, but have no specific goals for when you are forty, then there is no need to include anything in that life-stage box relating to your goals at forty.

Now that you have completed your 360 Vision Worksheet^{TM} and you are working off a common platform, you are ready to start defining your Home Culture through your vision, mission, and values statements (Steps 5, 6, and 7 in Life Management Strategy 1).

Special Bonus : This 360 Vision Worksheet^{TM} template as well as other templates that are used throughout the 5 Life Management Strategies can be downloaded at www.SmartBusinessThinkingatHome.com/bonus.

CASE STUDY 2: JANET & JAMES

Janet and James have recently started their life together. They have a blended family with grown kids from each of their respective first marriages. They both have jet-setting careers.

They have known that they have a lot going on, but their 360 Vision Worksheet^{TM} helped them to document what was swirling around in their minds and to deliberately consider and share areas of concern. Some of these included the emotional reality of "letting go" of their respective ailing parents in the years ahead, the growing independence of their children, the interdependence on their former spouses, the demands of their careers, and their personal aspirations.

Getting it all down on a couple sheets of paper really brought together all the different areas of their individual and joint lives and formed a common platform for them to plan their future.

STEP 5:
Defining your Home Culture - Vision

As a reminder, your vision statement is a statement of where you want to be in the future. While we may be familiar with vision statements in the work context, and perhaps even in an individual context, it is not yet commonplace for couples and families to go through the same transformative process. So you can consider yourself on the leading edge of thinking and as an innovator in this space!

In the corporate context, consider two examples of vision statements. Google's vision statement is "To develop a perfect search engine." While "perfect" is something that will never be achieved, as a vision statement it is motivational and clear in setting the bar high to strive for perfection. Another corporate example is Ocado, an online grocery retailer that has revolutionized grocery shopping in the UK. Their vision is to "…establish the first new supermarket in a generation." Again, another example of an inspiring statement that reflects their bold ambition to provide a radically different way of shopping.

Taking into consideration the work that you've already completed through your 360 Vision Worksheet^{TM}, you can now talk through your Family Vision statement and where you want to be in the future, based on a common understanding of your goals.

As you have this conversation you'll want to consider:

- Where do you want to be 5, 10, 20 years from now? (Individual and joint goals)

- What do you want your family's "legacy" to be? What do you want to be remembered for? What are your hopes for your children and their contributions to their loved ones and their community?

Typically, this is an exercise that many couples find difficult, in part because it's not something that they have considered before with any specificity. Most of us tend to live life largely reactively and tactically, or perhaps with some general ideas for the future. But to actually be explicit and choiceful in a phrase or a couple phrases that describes where you want to be in the future does require some work.

While, strictly speaking, you may want to try to be as concise as you can with your Family Vision (it is easier for you and others to remember punchy, short statements), our view is that if you need a couple statements to best reflect and capture your vision - go ahead and do so. It's your Family Vision Statement, and the main thing is for it to reflect what is important to you and to be something that motivates and guides you both and your family. We also believe that this should be something that can and should be shared with your family as this will help to make it real and bring it to life in your home.

Some examples of Family Vision Statements are:

- Be an inspiration for future generations in what we do and how we do it. Be passionate and proud about what we do (at home, corporately and socially).

- Leave a mark on our family tree/history while continuing the link of passing down traditions and creating new ones.

- Remain physically and mentally fit and active into old age.

- Develop children that become happy 40-year-olds - well educated, with positive attitudes, resilient to change, and grounded in strong values.

STEP 6:
Defining Your Home Culture - Mission

A mission statement is a statement of purpose that typically includes a goal and clarifies where to spend your energy (e.g., who we are and what we do).

In the corporate context, Google's mission is to "...organize the world's information and make it universally accessible and useful." This is a meaningful description of what they do. Ocado's mission is "To revolutionize the way people shop forever, by giving them a uniquely innovative and greener alternative to traditional grocery shopping." This is another example of a motivating and clear direction for their employees and other stakeholders to buy in to.

As you embark on your Family Mission Statement, you'll also want to consider your 360 Vision Worksheet™ and the conversations you have had in working through it. For some, the attainment of physical wealth and a strong work ethic may play a key role in defining their purpose. For others, it might be about life experiences and building lasting memories, or about family relationships and being good parents, siblings or children.

There is no right or wrong answer for your Family Mission Statement, and the process is part art and part science. You should choose it based on what seems right to you both and what reflects your joint view on what is important for you and your family. It should be motivating and needs to be something you can both buy into. The journey and conversations that you'll have through the process are as important as the output that you generate. You can always refine it going forwards, but it is important to do the work and record the best working version of your mission statement.

As you have this conversation, you'll want to consider:

- What and how ... What is your purpose as a family? How do you like to go about achieving it?
- What makes your family unique and special

Some examples of mission statements related to home life are:

- As a family, we double our joys and halve our burdens.

- We keep learning and improving ourselves, and have a positive impact in all that we do.

- We have a duty and are inspired to give back more than we have received.

STEP 7:
Defining your Home Culture - Values

Values are beliefs or principles that will help guide decision-making. Values are something that we develop inherently from our parents, our teachers, our friends, our environment. Sometimes we model what we see in others, sometimes we choose for ourselves based on our experiences. They implicitly guide the way we behave, what we deem is right or wrong, and where and how we choose to spend our time.

Corporate values, similar to vision and mission statements, are often distilled down to a manageable number (usually no more than about ten) and explicitly communicated to the organization to guide employees and other stakeholders to behave consistently within corporate norms. These may differ significantly from company to company and industry to industry.

Google's beliefs were crafted early on in their existence, but still have stood the test of time and reflect their culture. Beliefs like "You can be serious without a suit" or "Fast is better than slow" have guided and now reflect employee behavior.

Google's beliefs:

1. Focus on the user and all else will follow.

2. It's best to do one thing really, really well.

3. Fast is better than slow.

4. Democracy on the web works.
5. You don't need to be at your desk to need an answer.
6. You can make money without doing evil.
7. There's always more information out there.
8. The need for information crosses all borders.
9. You can be serious without a suit.
10. Great just isn't good enough.

Of the few families that I've encountered who have already made their values explicit and documented them, they have found it very valuable especially in communicating to children what is valued in their family. One mother said that she still had her handwritten page up on her wall even though her kids were teenagers. There is certainly something to be said about repetition and consistency! I've also seen lovely examples of values statements being printed, framed and displayed prominently at home to signal their importance and keep them front of mind.

As you have this conversation, you'll want to consider:

- What are your beliefs? What is important to you and your family?
- How can these beliefs and principles help to guide your decisions?

You may find it easiest to come up with a "long list" of values by each brainstorming separately and then coming together to see where there are similarities and differences, and then to rank the ones that you think will be the most effective in guiding the behaviors of your family. Some examples of family values are:

- We are kind

- We are a team
- We are polite
- We are respectful
- We share
- We look after our health
- We value differences
- We love learning & experiencing new things
- We don't sweat the small stuff
- We value doing things together as a couple and a family
- We've chosen only 1 corporate career - the other has flexibility
- We value experiences over accumulating "stuff"

An example of a completed vision, mission, and values statements is shown below. Enjoy creating one that reflects your family culture!

Family Vision, Mission, and Values - Example

1. Vision

Be an inspiration for future generations in what we do and how we do it. Being passionate and proud about what we do (at home, corporately, and socially).

Leaving a memorable mark on our family tree / history, while continuing the link of passing down traditions and creating new ones.

Physically and mentally fit and active into old age.

Happy children that are well educated, with positive attitudes, resilient to change, and grounded in strong values.

2. Mission

As a family, we double our joys and halve our burdens.

We keep learning and improving ourselves and have a positive impact in all that we do.

We have a duty and are inspired to give back more than we have received.

3. Values

- WE ARE KIND
- WE ARE A TEAM
- WE ARE POLITE
- WE ARE RESPECTFUL
- WE SHARE
- WE LOOK AFTER OUR HEALTH

- WE VALUE DIFFERENCES
- WE LOVE LEARNING & EXPERIENCING NEW THINGS
- WE DON'T SWEAT THE SMALL STUFF
- WE VALUE DOING THINGS TOGETHER AS A COUPLE AND A FAMILY

- WE'VE CHOSEN ONLY 1 CORPORATE CAREER - OTHER HAS FLEXIBILITY.
- PRIVATE EDUCATION IS THE PRIORITY OVER UPSIZING HOUSING
- WE VALUE EXPERIENCES OVER ACCUMULATING "STUFF"
- KEEP HOUSING SIMPLE - DOWNSIZE TO CONDO ONCE KIDS ARE GROWN TO MINIMIZE MAINTENANCE.

© 2011-2013 Copyright The Marriage Development Company Ltd. All rights reserved.   www.TheMarriageDevelopmentCompany.com

Congratulations on completing Life Management Strategy 1 and defining your Home Culture. We hope that the process of completing your Vision Worksheet and defining your Home Culture has helped to paint a common "big picture" that will be a solid foundation for navigating through both the strategic and more operational choices ahead.

Chapter Four Notes:
STRATEGY 1: DEFINING YOUR HOME CULTURE

Our **thoughts** and **next steps** from completing:

- Our 360 Vision Worksheet
- Our Vision, Mission, and Values Statements

Thoughts:

_____

_____

_____

_____

_____

_____

_____

_____

_____

_____

Next Steps:

Chapter Five

STRATEGY 2: AGREE YOUR 5-YEAR STRATEGIC PLAN

Strategic Plan. Mention strategic planning and most often we think of companies, boardrooms, consultants. Perhaps of complex, challenging choices, SWOT analyses and Porter's Five Forces. Or long, drawn out processes involving lots of people including blue-sky thinkers in their ivory tower, finance number crunchers, market researchers, product developers and marketers, amongst others.

Many companies have a formal strategic planning process that forces the concerted discipline of lifting our heads up from the day-to-day operational issues to take some time to consider longer-term issues of significant importance but that often would not get sufficient attention otherwise. Stephen Covey's 2x2 matrix of Importance vs. Urgency is a good reminder of how our days can be consumed by so many "urgent" items at the detriment of many "important" items. This chapter is about taking the time to plan for the mid- to long-term, an exercise that is vitally important, but very often is not urgent.

SMART BUSINESS THINKING AT HOME

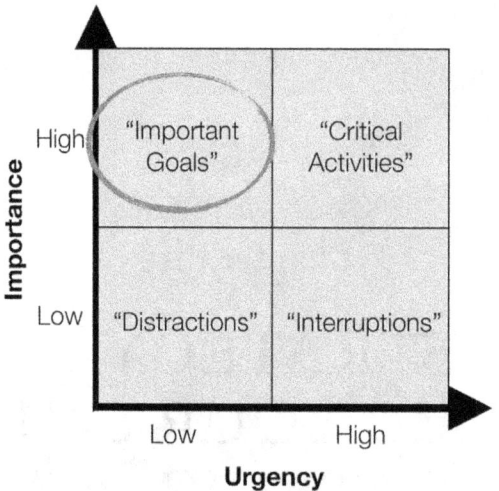

In a work context, the strategic planning process might consider things like key consumer trends over the next five years, competitive advantage in product offerings, plant sourcing options to remain cost competitive, talent management, key IT investments, macro factors including government or regulatory interventions, and various others. The glide path to key financial, consumer and other goals and the building blocks to achieve these goals is also defined. Typically, it is a process that involves input from various stakeholders and usually runs about halfway through the financial year to precede the annual planning process (thus setting the big picture that the next year's operational plans should help to deliver). So, if a company has a calendar year financial year, they might want to conduct their strategic planning towards the middle of the year (June or July) to then allow time for their annual planning process around September or October. This would allow for plans to be in place well in advance of the start of the next financial year again in January.

There are a few key elements in this strategic planning process that are important and translate to our home lives:

1. **Mid- to long-term time horizon:** It is so easy to get caught up in the reactive "busyness" of life and lose sight of the big

picture. It always seems to be such a revelation to couples when they start to look ahead 3 or 5 years or even longer. It helps as an alignment tool to have common end points or navigational beacons to guide along the way. Strategic planning by its nature usually assumes a 3-5 year horizon.

2. **Engagement of multiple stakeholders:** Strategic planning is rarely conducted by one individual sitting at their desk. It usually is facilitated by individuals, but draws upon input from all departments within the company: finance, marketing, sales, market research, product development, manufacturing, etc. Various departments and key stakeholders are usually engaged through the process to ensure there is proper input of information, but also to ensure that they will buy into the plan and thus enable the execution of the strategic plan. Often, there is significant debate, particularly on contentious issues, and this is a sign of good engagement through the process. Similarly, at home, communication between partners is critical to ensuring proper input, gaining buy-in and increasing the chances that ideas get executed without one party feeling left out of the loop. At times, we may tend to assume that our spouse may know or think as we do, which can lead to misunderstandings or sub-optimal solutions. There are many times when engaging your partner in a particular issue will yield a better solution than if you did it on your own. That is the essence of great teamwork! Similarly, if there are contentious issues, taking the time to discuss them openly and understanding each other's perspectives is important in staying together through the ups and downs of life.

3. **Explicit choices:** Part of the challenge of the strategic planning exercise is framing the right choices so that

decisions can be made. Sometimes, the most difficult part for an organization is to recognize what key choices are the most important ones to focus on and make. Is it a customer satisfaction issue, or a cost issue, or a skills gap issue? Ensuring the organization is spending its resources and management time on the right issues is critical. At home, it is as important to ensure that we are focusing on the right issues, that we agree what these are, and that we are spending our mental and emotional energies on working together to resolve these issues. It is equally important to ensure that the choices are framed explicitly and that decisions are then made from these. Sometimes decisions get made in life by "non- decisions," or you end up somewhere because you never made the explicit choice otherwise. This is precisely where strategic planning comes in. By having a process to annually look at the key choices for you as individuals, as a couple, and as a family that are coming up in the next five years, it is more likely that you will discuss these explicitly and come up with the right choices that take into consideration both of your inputs.

4. **Documented plan:** Strategic plans are formalized into a document that can be distributed, cascaded to key members of the organization, used as reference for tracking progress against and for developing next year's strategic plan. At home, it does not need to be a complex process, but it is important to document your strategic plan. The discipline of writing things down helps to ensure that you both have a similar take- away and are committed to one common plan. How often have you been in the situation at work where a colleague will nod their head in approval during a conversation, but once the plan is committed to paper and they are asked to sign off, then all the debate, questions

and concerns start to be aired? Committing to a plan on paper helps people engage and commit. And if there is disagreement, it is better to debate and resolve it at a planning stage, rather than at execution stage when there was an implicit understanding that you had both agreed to the plan.

STRATEGIC PLANNING FRAMEWORK

Now that you have an understanding of strategic planning, you can follow a strategic planning framework to create your own strategic plan at home.

A typical framework that is used in strategic planning is one that looks at three key questions:

1. Where are we today?
2. Where do we want to get to?
3. How are we going to get there?

Now, while these are relatively simple questions, they are high-level questions that help to distill down the key issues, distinguish the "forest from the trees," and frame the choices that need to be made. Let's look at each one in turn.

WHERE ARE WE TODAY?

While this may seem obvious, it is amazing how many versions of the "truth" exist in organizations. This may depend on what data you choose to believe or put weight on, who has provided the data, which department you are in and thus the relative importance you place on different issues, and what your objectives are, among others. We each have our own biases. The challenge is to cut through those biases to get to a common ground that all stakeholders agree is the current position. This is often where central departments in organizations play a role. They create a common definition and reporting system so that data can be comparable and is able to be aggregated.

For example, a company that is focused on customer satisfaction will need a common way of measuring this across product areas and geographies. Otherwise, managers for Product or Service A would have no way of comparing their results versus from the manager of Product B. It's also where common culture is important - so that you are speaking the same "language" and considering the same areas to be important. For example, if the culture of the company is one with advanced HR policies and values its employees, employee retention issues might be an area for focused improvement. However, if the company is used to a transient workforce and has a good pipeline of new workers, this may be less of an issue. The critical first step in the strategic planning process is to create this common fact base and starting point that is accepted as the current state.

> IT IS SO EASY TO GET CAUGHT UP IN THE REACTIVE "BUSYNESS" OF LIFE AND LOSE SIGHT OF THE BIG PICTURE.

Similarly at home, depending on what you value, you might consider things to be or not to be of significance. Take, for example, keeping a tidy house. Perhaps one of you likes to maintain a very tidy house. However, your spouse might not mind some disorder and may not see this as an issue. If this is of significant enough concern to one of you, it should be captured within the "Where you are today?" section. There may then be choices to be made - do you dedicate more time to cleaning and tidying, do you hire a cleaner and fund it from another area like fewer meals out, or do you leave it as is?

There may be several areas where you may have different perceptions of what the current situation is. Perhaps relating to finances - are we spending too much, or are we not earning enough? Other example areas where you may have differing views of the current state include whether you are spending too much time with your in-laws, whether your children are signed up to too many activities, or whether you are spending enough time together as a couple. The list can go on and on. The question is whether you both have a common view (and if even there are differences, at least acknowledging these) of where you are today and what the key issues are as well as what progress you have made against them.

Evaluating "Where are we today?" across various categories of your life and agreeing on this starting point is the important first step.

Where do we want to get to?

Now that you have a common view of where you are today, the next step is to make some choices about where you want to be in the future. For the purpose of this strategic planning exercise, let's consider five years from now. That is enough time to bring about significant change in key areas, but within the horizon that you can focus on implementation.

Here is where you start to make some choices about your dreams and desires, but grounded with the reality of today's situation. By taking a view across the various categories in your life, you will also be forced to prioritize to ensure that your plan remains realistic. It is important, though, to acknowledge your dreams and desires, as these will become your change catalysts and will help you to prioritize your energy and resources to help make them happen. By agreeing them together, you'll be working towards them together - a journey together to a common destination.

Perhaps one of you has the goal of running a marathon or climbing Mount Everest. To achieve this, you'll need time to train, which means less time for other things, including spending time with your family. If this is agreed as a key activity within your strategic plan, you'll have the commitment of your partner and perhaps can even make it a memorable event for the whole family. For example, the entire family can participate in some of the training and events and support the achievement of this goal. By contrast, if this is an individual goal, decided unilaterally and without input from your partner, there may be resentment due to the time away from the family and tolerance rather than embracing it as a common goal.

Another choice might be around finances. One spouse might have the desire to make pre- payments towards your mortgage to reduce it by one quarter over the next five years. Agreeing this goal might require foregoing holidays or reducing expenditures in other areas in the short- term - clearly an area that will impact the whole family. But the long-term benefit of this may be something you agree on. Perhaps this may enable pursuing an alternate career with a lower salary but greater satisfaction and more flexibility for time at home. Again, this a choice worth considering and discussing that will have considerable impact on the whole family.

There are also some choices that might be a result of things outside our control. Take, for example, looking after ailing parents. While we can't control the timing for ill health, it is something that we can have contingency plans for. We can also acknowledge that the time we have with healthy parents and relatives as they age is limited, and there may be some things that we would like to do with them or for them.

Another example is teenagers that are growing up quickly and will soon be away at college. You may want to plan what key memories you want to build with them before they leave home. The list can go on and on. The point is that you need to take the time to think further ahead than just next week or next month to be able to put the focus on making your goals happen. By agreeing on your five-year strategy, you will adjust your "navigation" to steer towards your goals. Just going about the same day-to-day tasks may not get you there, and the opportunity may be lost.

It is, however, important to acknowledge again that things do change. That is life. There may be something unexpected that happens in the five years that means that you have a new priority in your life and are not able to achieve all your initial goals. That's okay and it's right to adjust your plans to reflect this. Life is dynamic and your plans need to be flexible enough to reflect this. There are also things which are just out of our control. The benefit, though, is that when these unexpected events happen, at least you are working from a common understanding of what you originally wanted to achieve. Perhaps it's illness, or an unexpected job move, or a late pregnancy - these things happen. In reality, change happens in companies as well and they also have to adjust their plans. It is much better to have a plan that you can update than to have none at all. So while you wouldn't expect all your mid- to long-term choices to change drastically every year, there will be some change and adjustments that you can make to the following year's strategic plan.

How are we going to get there?

The final step, then, once you have made the choices of where you want to get to, is to determine how you are going to get there. This might include specific actions that need to be accomplished for implementation - perhaps some that fall on your shoulders and some on your spouse's. Or perhaps you may need to acquire new skills to help enable your goals - for example, retraining for a career change within five years.

This step grounds your strategic choices in the reality of implementation and forces you to consider the gap between where you are today and where you want to get to. You then need to build the bridge from the current situation to your five-year plans. It will provide insight on just how much change is required and perhaps be a reality check on whether your choices are consistent and achievable. Particularly if you have made various choices that require change across different categories in your life, you will need to determine whether you have the capacity to deliver them all within the next five years - in terms of time, energy and money. Being realistic and prioritizing goals will help to keep you on track. If you find that you've taken on too much, then agree to the top priorities and recognize that some others may fall into years further out (if they are not time-sensitive) or may be abandoned altogether. In the context of strategic planning at work, it is common to have too many priorities at the start of the process - often as a result of each department having their own pet projects. These usually then go through a prioritization funnel exercise - usually based on how much value can be attributed to each as well as the strategic imperative of each. This prioritization then enables shared and scarce resources to be allocated appropriately and with consideration (e.g., IT resources, funding, skilled managers, etc.). While it may not be possible to measure "value" at home as the means of prioritizing, the principle of trying to agree on some form of prioritization that you can both agree to is still relevant and helpful.

Following is an example of a high-level corporate strategic plan:

Developing your 5-year strategic plan at home

Step 1:
Choose the key life categories to include in your strategic plan

Use the same key categories you considered for your 360 Vision Worksheet™ to take a comprehensive look at your home life. Again, feel free to tailor these and add others to reflect any additional key categories in your life.

As a reminder, the key categories identified earlier are: Self, Spouse, Family, Career, Health, Personal Development, Finance & Property, Travel & Visitors, Entertainment, Spiritual Growth.

We have found that using the prompts of these different categories ensures that we consider life as a whole rather than the individual elements of it that may happen to be top of mind.

You can then set up your template with your chosen categories as the rows of your table. Remember these templates can also be downloaded at www.SmartBusinessThinkingatHome.com/bonus.

Step 2:
Where are we today?

This step is about setting a common starting point. While you may assume that you both agree what the current status is, it's worth double checking. Often, our perceptions may not necessarily be consistent with what that of our spouse's. And while this step may seem trivial to some, it is very important; if you don't agree on the starting point, then you'll have different views on how to get to the end point of your goals.

This is as true in business as it is at home. Take the example of a business unit where sales have been declining. One manager may believe that sales are declining due to a decrease in advertising spending. Another might believe that they are declining because competitors have reduced their pricing. And yet another manager might believe it is because of product quality issues. Clearly, in this example, there is no agreement on the current status quo and hence each manager will likely choose a different solution to the goal of increasing sales.

Similarly, at home, one of you might feel that your finances are fine because you are managing to cover your monthly household costs without borrowings. The other spouse might feel that your finances are not fine because you are not saving anything towards your retirement. It's important to acknowledge your different starting points. It is also helpful to ensure that you have a common view of key data or your fact-base - for example, what your joint household income and expenses are, in this case.

In the area of health, one of you might be feeling overweight, out of shape and generally burnt out from work. By talking through each category and each of your views on "Where are we today?" you will make each other aware of your perceptions and pave the way for a joint path forwards. It's okay for you to have different starting points. The point of this exercise is to communicate them to each other and to have a common awareness of them.

Use the template and the key categories to prompt your conversation as you fill out the first column related to "Where are we today?". The idea is to synthesize in a few key bullet points the essence or key information (rather than writing an essay for each). This will then form the basis for the choices that you frame in the next section - so ensure that these are comprehensive.

STEP 3:
Where do we want to get to?

In Step 3, you build on the areas you identified in Step 2, "Where we are today," and think about where you'd like to be five years from now. You may have touched on some of these when doing your 360 Vision Worksheet™ in the previous chapter. If so, that's a great starting point for then having more in-depth discussions on choices you may need to make.

Take the example of saving for retirement. You may agree that in the next five years you want to start saving towards your retirement and that you will start saving 5% of your income to do this.

Or you may have friends who have moved away from your neighborhood and who you are starting to lose touch with. You may decide that there are two couples or families that five years from now you want to have re-established the close friendship with.

Or, in the example of saving for a down payment on a property, you may say that five years from now you want to have purchased your home and have a mortgage of no more than $X.

Again, capture your thoughts in bullet points and try to be as specific and concise as you can. Repeat this for all the key areas you have identified.

STEP 4:
How are we going to get there?

In this final step, you'll build the bridge between where you are today and where you want to get to.

So in the example of friends that you want to be close with five years from now, you may say that you will make the effort to see them twice a year and to stay in touch with the children through birthday/holiday cards and gifts.

And in the example of saving for a down payment for your home, you may determine that at your current savings rate you will not be able to purchase the home that you would like to be in five years from now. You may then say that to get there in five years you need to double your savings rate, and consider the impact of that decision.

As you review each area of importance you have identified, you may need to prioritize as it may not be realistic to do everything that you initially set out to do. There may not be enough time or money or energy to do it all. So then, you need to prioritize and get to a single plan that you agree on.

So, for example, the desire to run a marathon might compete for time with the visits with friends that you'd like to keep in touch with. Perhaps you agree to phase things, so that your focus as a family for the first two years until the race is to support the marathon runner and that in that period you'll make do with keeping in touch with your distant friends over the phone regularly and in person once a year. After the marathon, you would plan to spend increased time with them.

As in life, there will likely be some give and take, as there will be some areas that you agree are of importance and then others that may be more important to one or the other of you. The most important thing is to be aware of these similarities and differences and to talk them through. This framework helps to facilitate those conversations that may be difficult to have or may not otherwise happen.

Congratulations on completing Life Management Strategy 2 and agreeing on your 5-Year Strategic Plan. These first two Life Management Strategies consider a mid- to long-term horizon to help to set a joint navigational compass of where you are heading. Life Management Strategies 3 and 4 will focus on prioritization and operational choices for the year ahead.

Chapter Five Notes:
STRATEGY 2: AGREE YOUR 5-YEAR STRATEGIC PLAN

Our **thoughts** and **next steps** from completing:

- Our 5-year Strategic Plan

Thoughts:

_____
_____
_____
_____
_____
_____
_____
_____
_____
_____

Next Steps:

Chapter Six

STRATEGY 3: MEMORIZE YOUR 3-5 ANNUAL PRIORITIES

A NNUAL PRIORITIES ARE, more simply put, priorities for the year ahead. They are the top three to five most important activities across an organization for the year ahead. You may ask why we suggest you memorize them. Well, if you memorize them, it's a pretty good guarantee that you are aware of them, have them on the top of your mind, and will consider them in your daily decisions and behaviors. And why only have three to five of them? This forces us to be choiceful and ensures that we spend enough time, energy and resources on these very limited priorities, rather than spreading ourselves too thin and in the end accomplishing very little.

In the context of companies, selecting limited key priorities across the organization ensures that there are company-wide priorities that unify the firm and leverage its full scale and resources. It enables trade-offs and resource prioritization, taking into consideration the broadest context rather than a narrow view. And importantly, it also recognizes what is less of a priority and thus what will not get done in the year ahead. There is always the temptation to try to get everything done, but in the process of saying yes to everything, often nothing gets done properly, or the most important activities don't get the attention they deserve.

In the case of for-profit companies, the priorities tend to be the highest value-creating activities or perhaps those of greatest strategic importance. Sometimes these priorities are referred to as the "management agenda" or "key priorities."

Take for example a company that has various product lines - let's say in the chocolate category. The product development department may have developed five different product improvements for various product lines. For example: extra crunchy, a new dark chocolate version, better packaging, a gifting version, etc. However, the sales department might only be able to launch one properly for the year to ensure there is the appropriate distribution and promotion in-store. Also, the advertising budget for the category might also only fund one launch campaign. If a different manager is responsible for each chocolate upgrade, they might each be tempted to promote their own launch, which might marginally improve each of their respective business lines. An alternative would be to conduct a prioritization exercise to determine which upgrade would be most beneficial for the company to launch that year and thus be the focus for the sales force and advertising department.

There may also be the choice to enter into a new geography and this may be competing for resources along with the product upgrade. Or perhaps there is the opportunity to develop the online direct-to-consumer channel. All these are possible ways to create value and will need to go through some prioritization to distill down the key activities that will require focus this year (and also consequently, those that will not have the focus).

Typically, a prioritization process would identify candidate priority areas from across the organization (e.g., this might be to launch product X, or to improve customer service Y, or to invest in emerging market Z). Once this "long list" is developed, a common fact base will be developed which might pull together existing data and analysis and identify areas for further analysis. Criteria for then prioritizing will be determined and applied. Typically, this would be based on value creation, perhaps with some adjustment for the risk of realizing the potential. And then the debate begins - as it is equally important to have robust discussion and apply judgment and intuition to the analysis in coming to a conclusion.

The benefit of going through this process is that it provides clarity to all involved and allows teams to work together to execute on agreed plans, rather than having the friction that might result from ambiguity over whose plan is more important that than the other.

> QUITE OFTEN, THERE IS NO EXPLICIT CONVERSATION ABOUT WHAT THE KEY FAMILY PRIORITIES ARE.

This is also why it can be so beneficial in the home context. Quite often, there is no explicit conversation about what the key family priorities are for the year ahead. As a result of this ambiguity at the planning stage, couples may end up working at cross purposes and/or feeling that they weren't consulted or don't agree with where time, energy and money are being spent. By agreeing on the key priorities and themes for the year, it is easier to be aligned through the day-to-day execution.

For example, you might decide that your joint key priorities for the year ahead are:

1. Grow Spouse A's career
2. Settle Child B in school
3. Downsizing elderly parent's home

By explicitly selecting these upfront, any activities related to these priorities now float to the top of both of your priority lists. So when Spouse A needs to spend extra time traveling for work or preparing for that key client meeting, it's okay because it's an agreed upon priority. It'll be something that both of you are interested in and supporting each other on. Similarly, if Child B isn't settling well in school, you'll have it on the top of your mind to arrange playdates, or extra tutoring, or whatever might help the situation. Finally, for the priority of downsizing an elderly parent's home, acknowledging it as a priority will ensure that you are dedicating sufficient time and energy to helping find alternative solutions - whether it is a smaller place for your parents to live or renovations to your home to accommodate them living with your family.

Another example of annual priorities might be:

1. Health and exercise for Spouse B to reduce weight and get fit

2. More quality time with friends

3. Optimizing financial planning & investments

To select your priorities, you should consider the following criteria for them:

- Choiceful - Frame your choices concisely enough that by selecting your priorities you are also by definition closing down alternatives. For example, "Looking after the children" is too vague and may mean different things to each of you.

- Explicit - Discuss all candidate ideas openly and explicitly, rather than keeping pet projects implicit. Once you have selected your priorities, make sure you write them down.

- Prioritized - Rank your top choices so that you can select your joint top 3 to 5 choices. You may carry the ones that didn't make the short list forward as candidates for the next year.

- Agreed - While this may seem obvious, sometimes a distracted head nod does not translate to real agreement and commitment. Make sure you have taken the time to have a good conversation and that you are both committed to these top 3 to 5 priorities for the year ahead.

DEVELOPING YOUR TOP 3 TO 5 ANNUAL PRIORITIES AT HOME

STEP 1:
Identify your long list of candidate priorities separately

Take the time to each write down on a sheet of paper what you consider to be the most important priorities for the year ahead. Give yourselves at least ten minutes to complete this exercise individually (without comparing notes yet). We suggest that you try to prioritize within your individual lists the ones that are the most important priorities to you.

STEP 2:
Share and discuss your candidate ideas to come up with a joint long list

As you talk through your individual lists and why each item was important to you, you may bounce ideas off each other and come up with new priorities or amend current ones.

For example, when we did this exercise one year, my husband had cleaning the house and "de-cluttering" as one of his priorities, which was nowhere to be seen on my list! However, after talking about it in more detail, I came to understand that it was a matter of sanity for him to have a tidy house, as he isn't able to concentrate if there is clutter around him. We then re-categorized this under Health (as mental health!), which was a category that I understood and could commit to as being a priority. This process took one of my husband's priorities that otherwise would not have been so meaningful to me and repositioned it into something that was very easy for me to have at the top of our joint list.

At the end of Step 2, you will have your agreed on long list of priorities.

STEP 3:
Prioritize your joint list to select your top 3 to 5 priorities for the year ahead

Once you have your long list, you can now start your selection process for your top 3 to 5 priorities. Select your 3 to 5 priorities individually and then mark up the list or write them down individually. This will make it clear where you have consensus and where there is difference. Talk this through and try to get to a joint position on your top 3 to 5 priorities. Write them down and repeat them frequently until you both have them committed to memory.

Try to be realistic about what you can achieve in a given year, particularly if your priorities will stretch you in terms of money or time. Don't be afraid to agree that there will be things that won't get done - perhaps the renovations or the holiday to Greece or the extra course you wanted to take. Save those thoughts. Keep your notes and bring them back next year when you are going through the process again.

These 3 to 5 top priorities should remain at the forefront of your thoughts throughout the year, so don't be shy to quiz each other playfully to make sure that you've got them committed to memory. They need to be on the top of your mind to ensure that your day-to- day behaviors and implicit allocation of time or reaction to situations is reflecting these priorities.

Congratulations on completing Life Management Strategy 3 and defining your Top 3-5 Annual Priorities. This is one of our favorite strategies – perhaps because of its simplicity but also because of the explicit and implicit benefits we consistently reap from having aligned high-level priorities and an explicit agreement of where we are focusing our energy, time, and money for the year ahead. It pre-empts so many discussions or potential disagreements and keeps us on the "front foot" and working together on life projects we both have prioritized.

Chapter Six Notes:
STRATEGY 3: MEMORIZE YOUR 3-5 KEY ANNUAL PRIORITIES

Our **thoughts** and **next steps** from completing:

- Our 3-5 Key Annual Priorities

Thoughts:

_____

_____

_____

_____

_____

_____

_____

_____

_____

_____

_____

_____

Next Steps:

Chapter Seven

STRATEGY 4: DETAIL YOUR ANNUAL OPERATING PLAN

AN OPERATING PLAN focuses on the short-term allocation of resources - primarily people's time and energy. It tends to focus on the year ahead, unlike your strategic plan, which has a longer time horizon. It also is consistent with the investment choices that have been made and perhaps been documented in a corresponding financial plan.

So the operating plan is really about getting stuff done this year, but getting stuff done in a coordinated and synergistic way that adds up to a whole that's greater than the sum of the parts. And all these activities will also reflect the choices that you have made on the Key Priorities for the year.

Having a unified plan is so important because it is easy for different divisions or departments to get caught up in their own "silo" of a plan - formulating their plans without properly consulting, communicating and engaging other departments that may be critical to the success of their interdependent plans. In the end there is a risk that, despite a lot of busyness and work going on, the activities may not deliver the desired impact because they rely on resources from other departments that have not been committed. This may be true across departments like sales or customer service or product development or marketing or IT.

Take for example a product launch where the advertising department is working hard to develop an ad for the launch date. If the sales department isn't working toward the same priorities to then get the new product in store and supported with in-store features or promotions, then the cumulative benefit of having the consumer see the ad and then walk into the store to find and buy the product will not be achieved. The investment in the advertising media to generate awareness will not be able to translate into increased sales if the sales department hasn't managed to get the product onto enough retailers' shelves. If both departments had been involved in a joint planning process, they would have committed to an agreed launch date and would have then based their respective plans on activities that would help support this.

Or perhaps there are hand-offs in a project amongst team members that aren't always handled effectively. So perhaps you are waiting for some consumer research from your market research department for a crucial client presentation. The meeting date was then pulled forward in the calendar but never communicated to the market research team and thus the research is coming in too late, after your make-or-break client meeting. Coordination across broader teams takes a lot of effort and requires skill, enablers, and a culture of teamworking to be done effectively. That's because business (and life also) is dynamic – things change. It's often hard enough to get everyone to agree to a single initial plan, but that is only half the effort. The plan then changes with time, and ensuring that there is a mechanism to keep everyone informed of the constantly changing context is critical to having all parts of the team working together. How often have you spent time working on some aspect of a project only to find out that something has changed, or a decision has been made that means that your work is no longer relevant? If you could have been informed at the point the change happened, then you would have been able to re-invest your time and energy into a value- creating activity. Keeping all the moving parts moving in the right direction is pretty impossible to do in an ad-hoc manner. This is where the operating plan comes in, along with the cycle to reflect changes over the year.

The broad steps in the cycle include:

1. **Planning** - Developing the plan with the relevant stakeholders' input and an agreed upon process for how the plan will be decided (i.e. who makes the final decision or who will provide input).

2. **Documenting** - As the plan is being iterated and once it has been agreed upon, it needs to be documented explicitly so that there is a common understanding and less room for misunderstanding. This can be communicated at different levels - perhaps a high-level documentation with the most important key activities in the plan, with more detailed sub-levels for greater clarity on implementation (e.g., quarterly, monthly or weekly planning).

3. **Implementation & Monitoring** – Things will inevitably change between planning and implementation. Either activities won't get delivered to plan or timing or changes to the original plan will be needed. An agreed implementation and monitoring process will usually inform the plan owners when things are off track or when additional decisions need to be made.

The cycle will then repeat itself with re-planning to reflect changes (in- year changes will likely be less weighty than the original planning decisions, but still need to be considered to update the plan and ensure everyone is working off of the latest version).

Let's look at an example of a high-level annual plan for an organization.

Note that we have divided the year into quarters, which we feel is about the right level of granularity for planning at home without getting lost in the detail. If you really want to get into the detail you could take it down to a monthly level - just make sure you don't lose sight of the forest for the trees!

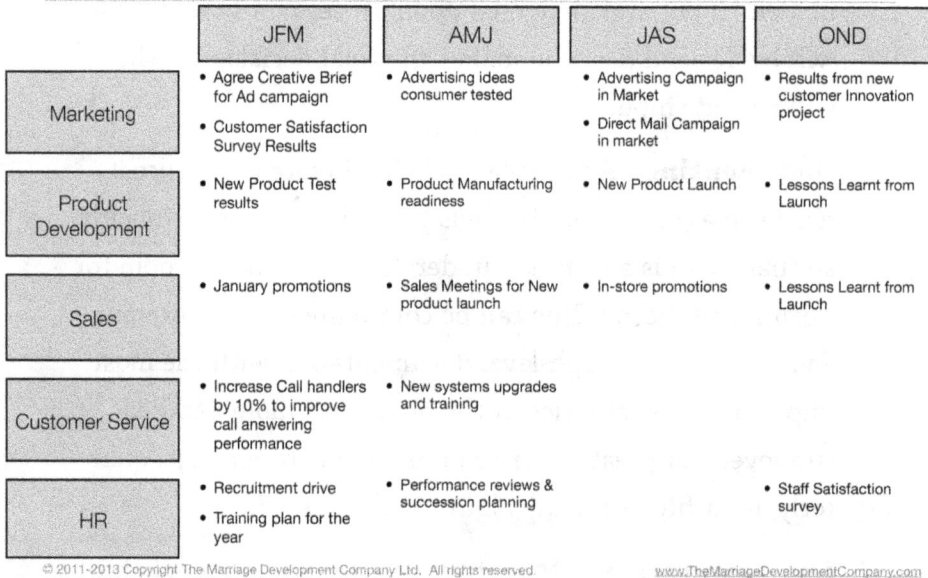

So in this example we are looking at the key plans across marketing, product development, sales, customer service and HR. Assume that one of the key priorities for this company is to launch product X in July. You can see that this is then reflected in each of the department plans. Marketing has a plan to have advertising and direct mail ready in the 3rd quarter (July to September). Product development's plan reflects the July launch and the work that needs to precede it (product test results and manufacturing readiness). Sales has planned for in-store promotions in July and has scheduled their sales meetings for quarter 2 (April to June) to "sell-in" the new product. Customer service has increased their call handlers and introduced new systems and training in advance of the

July product launch. We can see that all these departments are working synergistically towards the same key priority.

ANNUAL OPERATING PLAN AT HOME

So, how does this all work at home? Well, at home, just as at work, we are part of a team that needs to work together to get things done. If we work together well then we get a lot done and have fun in the process, and if we don't work together so well then it seems difficult to get stuff done and there is lots of working at cross purposes, re-work, and friction in our day-to-day.

The purpose of introducing an Annual Operating Plan at home is to help to coordinate your efforts towards key activities that you will have jointly agreed. The process, by its nature, will enable communication and help to map or phase activities in an implementable way. By stepping back and looking at the upcoming year as a whole, you can more easily see relative priorities and choose where to spend your time and energy.

Also, we'll show you how by following this process you can easily get to sixty key activities that you have both agreed to - and that's even before the year starts! That means sixty activities that you will work together or support each other on, and sixty fewer things to disagree on in the heat of the moment during the year.

Finally, the way you go about developing, documenting, implementing and monitoring your Annual Plan should reflect an approach that you feel comfortable with and can call your own. If you like operating at a high level, then, by all means, conduct the planning at a high level as we illustrate here. If you are both project managers and love Excel and the detail and want to work towards a monthly plan, then by all means, go ahead. Also, with respect to the review sessions, we think that quarterly is about right for most people (so three review sessions before you plan your next year). At a minimum, you should have a mid-year review (at least one review session before planning the next year), but if you feel that you want to review your plan more often (particularly if there are key time-sensitive activities that you are trying to monitor) then you should feel free to do so. Also these "reviews" should be positive, enjoyable, and fun as you are working together on things that are important to you.

How do we develop our Annual Operating Plan at home?

You have already completed the first 3 Life Management Strategies that start off with the big strategic picture and start to narrow down to more "nitty gritty" areas. As part of Life Management Strategy 3, you defined your Key Annual Priorities. You should keep these in mind as you identify the various activities in your Operating Plan and ensure that these reflect and support the key priorities you have identified for your year.

As we did in the previous exercises, we will take a 360-degree look at the various areas of your life and then identify the key activities by quarter for each of your life categories. This time we will do so with a one year time horizon in mind.

60 Agreed Activities

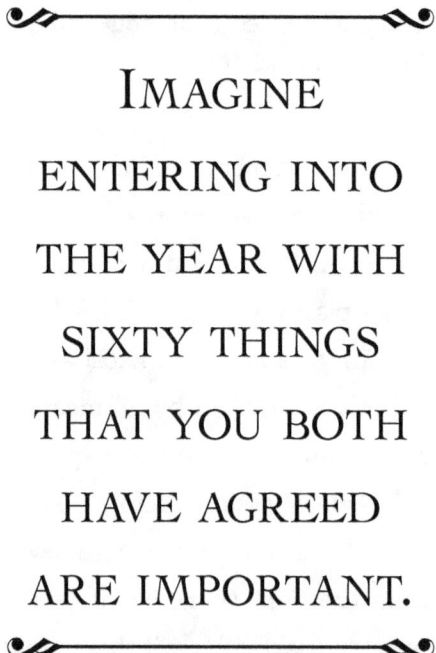

Imagine entering into the year with sixty things that you both have agreed are important.

We're going to use a similar approach to what we saw in the business example - we'll divide up the year into quarters. Again, that gets it granular enough that it is clear what needs to be done when, but you're not swimming in detail (unless that is what you like!). So consider four quarters in the year and then, say, five key life categories that you have chosen. That forms a 4x5 matrix of twenty different elements. Now

Strategy 4: Detail Your Annual Operating Plan

consider that you can identify three key activities for each of these and agree that they are important to get done. Twenty elements times three key activities each gives sixty activities that you have agreed to do.

What a great start in getting aligned for the year ahead! Imagine entering into the year with sixty things that you both have agreed are important and will get done. That means less things to decide "on the fly" during the year, and potentially fewer things to disagree on!

And because you have worked together to define these sixty activities, you've had great conversations in the process that have helped you understand your relative priorities and perspectives that will further help as you move into the implementation and monitoring phase of the cycle.

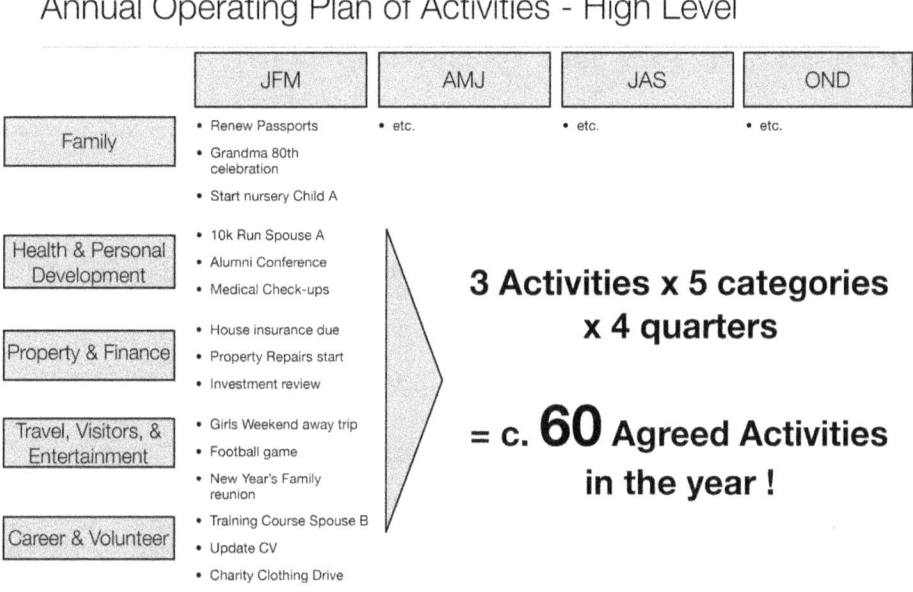

Sometimes it takes granular, meaningful conversations to really understand what is important to each of us and why. It's a give and take process, but at the end of it there's a single plan that you have both committed to for the year ahead. That's a great achievement.

71

STEP 1:
Choose your Life Categories and set up your template

Set up your framework so you know how you are going to develop the plan. While it may seem out of date, we suggest that you start off by using a pen and paper. This makes it easy for you to have a conversation together and not get bogged down in word-smithing a document that one of you is typing into your laptop. We find that pen and paper also facilitates a more equal and open process where either of you can take the pen and jot down your thoughts on the paper.

You can simply set up four columns that represent each quarter of the year. Typically, we suggest planning about a quarter in advance. So if it's about September, that's the perfect time to start planning for the calendar year ahead. You can use as your headings:

Q1(Jan-Mar), Q2 (Apr-Jun), Q3 (Jul-Sep), Q4 (Oct-Dec).

If you are starting your planning at a different point in the year, you can make the decision to plan for the next calendar year, or for the current or next quarter - that's up to you. So, for example, if you start your planning in April, you might want to start your planning for the year period starting in July and ending next June:

Q3 (Jul-Sep), Q4 (Oct-Dec), Q1 (Jan-Mar), Q2 (Apr-Jun)

Either way is fine, as long as you both agree it.

Now that you've set up the headers for your columns, you can start to choose the Life Categories for your rows. You'll probably want to use the same ones that you selected for your Strategic Plan earlier.

Below are the original ones that we had suggested, but that you may have tailored:

Self, Spouse, Family, Career, Health, Personal Development, Finance & Property, Travel & Visitors, Entertainment, Spiritual Growth, Others.

So, now with your column headers and rows defined - you are all set to start with the planning!

STEP 2:
Create and document your plan -
What needs to happen and When

As you review each Life Category in your rows, you will start to identify key activities within each. Capture each activity within the time of the year that it needs to get done. As you start to populate your plan, you'll be able to see perhaps some conflicts (too many visitors coming around the same time of the year) or perhaps some activities that need to be done at a specific point in the year (family photo for Christmas cards or home repairs while you are away on summer holidays, etc.). That is part of the process of developing your plan. Keep talking and keep writing/revising until you both feel that you've captured the key activities for each Life Category.

After you have filled out your plan, you'll want to do a check back to the Key Annual Priorities that you agreed to ensure that the plan you've developed reflects these.

Once you have your written plan agreed and have had the great conversations getting there, you may now want to transfer this to an electronic file which you can then save.

If you agreed three activities for each of the five Life Categories across four quarters of the year, you'll now have your 60 agreed activities! If you are there or thereabouts, that's a great achievement.

STEP 3:
Agree your review and revision process

Finally, last but not least, is agreeing how often you are going to review your Annual Operating plan and when. If you have agreed to a quarterly review, then set these dates in your calendar as a reminder. We tend to do it over a meal together - reviewing our original plan and using the Red / Amber / Green traffic light system. Items that have been completed in the quarter get highlighted green. Those that are in-progress and on-track but not yet delivered are amber. And those off-track are highlighted red.

We can then easily see what needs a bit more focus for the quarter ahead. Take the example of passport renewals that perhaps didn't get done when the passports were going to expire as noted in the original plan - it's now highlighted as a red item, and depending on our travel plans might become very urgent or something that we just need to keep in mind to get done soon.

Remember, reviewing and revising your plan isn't meant to be threatening – and should always be done in the spirit of working together and enjoying working together! Change happens and things sometimes don't get done. But let's stay together on why and therefore what we need to do about it. Perhaps you had a bout of flu in the family and so nothing got done for a month - at least you both know why and agree how the plan should be changed. It's much more about staying on the same page as things change in the plan so that you avoid misunderstandings down the road. It's also about reprioritizing in a way that you've both committed to. Perhaps your parents are now coming to visit for a month - so you'll want to agree what won't get done because you'll be spending time together with them.

And finally, these should be productive and fun sessions because you'll be celebrating all that you have accomplished and also what you still want to accomplish. It's being purposeful about where and how you spend your time so that you can achieve the activities you've both agreed as being the most important for the year.

Congratulations on completing Life Management Strategy 4 - Detailing your Annual Operating Plan. You have now completed your "big picture" through Life Management Strategies 1 & 2 and have also prioritized and planned for the year ahead in Life Management Strategies 3 & 4. We hope that through this process you have had good conversations and have enjoyed working together on your plans. This process is one of dreaming together but also being balanced in the day-to-day realities of life. The final Life Management Strategy – Strategy 5 will look at some key elements to decision making.

Chapter Seven Notes:
STRATEGY 4: DETAIL YOUR ANNUAL OPERATING PLAN

Our **thoughts** and **next steps** from completing:

- Our Annual Operating Plan

Thoughts:

_____

_____

_____

_____

_____

_____

_____

_____

_____

_____

_____

Next Steps:

Chapter Eight

STRATEGY 5: AGREE THE "WHAT" AND "WHO" OF DECISIONS

MAKING DECISIONS IS something that we all do many times a day. Sometimes we make them based on habit; they are based on what we've always done before. Sometimes we labor over them and pour over reams and reams of data and hold many meetings before making them. Sometimes we make them on a whim just because that's what feels right. And sometimes we even avoid making decisions, but in doing so by default decide to continue with the status quo.

Decisions big and small - life is full of them. We make them at work and we make them at home.

So what is a decision? We like to say that making a decision is: "Making a choice from several possible implicit or explicit alternatives."

There is always a choice involved. And to make a choice there needs to be alternatives. Sometimes, however, these alternatives are not explicit and so we may not be aware that there is a choice to be made, or we might not have considered one or more of the alternatives in our decision-making.

Sometimes we need others' buy-in to the decision for it to be implemented, but may have overlooked them in the decision-making process

Sometimes we don't have enough information or the right type of information. These are just a few of the reasons why decision-making is often challenging.

Various common "defects" in business decisions were highlighted in a Business Week article[5] that we have found very relevant to broader "life" decisions:

- Decisions don't get made: There's the continual study of unresolved issues

- Decisions appear to have been made but then fall apart

- Decisions get made, but follow-up action isn't timely: The decision- making process is followed by a time-consuming "buy-in" process

- Decisions get made, but they're bad

If we consider each of the above defects in the context of decisions made at home, we can find that they are equally relevant. For example, how easy is it to postpone difficult decisions that perhaps we'll never have enough information to help us decide - perhaps whether to take the leap into a new career path or whether to proceed with IVF. Or how often have we apparently jointly "decided" to do something, only to find that our partner doesn't recall ever having agreed to such a deed? Or how often can you look at a life decision and say that it was a probably a bad decision that you made - whether it was a medical test you put off for too long or a dream that you never took the time to fulfill?

When we consider how many big decisions we have or will still have to make in life, it's no surprise that there will be "defects" in some of these decisions we make. After all, decision-making is part art and part science. This makes it sometimes tricky, especially when the decisions are not just

---

5   "Why Decisions Need Design", BusinessWeek, Roger Martin, 30 August 2005.

ours to make, but ones that need the involvement of our partner and perhaps other stakeholders as well. Some of these decisions might include

- Career decisions/changing jobs
- Whether to relocate or change homes - proactively or reactively
- Having kids/adoption/IVF
- Medical treatment decisions
- Financial decisions - how much to spend/save, when to retire, where to invest
- Having parents/in-laws live with you
- Choices in parenting and raising children

And these are just a few of the big, really life-changing ones. When you consider all the other smaller decisions we make day in and day out, it seems to make some sense to try to apply some best practices to help improve the process around decision-making and hopefully the quality of these decisions.

We are going to take a look at both what decisions need to be made and who needs to make them.

WHAT DECISIONS NEED TO BE MADE?

Part of the challenge at home is ensuring that there is a common view of what decisions are coming up and need to be made. We call this your "Decision Radar." If you need to make a decision, it's always helpful if you know that you need to make it! Sounds obvious, and perhaps if it is a decision that you are making on your own, you will implicitly be aware of it. However, if it is something on your partner's mind, it may be totally off your radar. Have you ever heard comments like "Nobody told me that" or "Do we have to talk about that now?" coming from your partner when you approach them with what may seem like an obvious decision that needs to be made? Perhaps we need to decide where to go for summer holidays in the next week so that we can take advantage of lower fares. Or we need to decide if we are going ahead with the home renovations that we've had on the back burner. Or we need to finally decide whether we will work through a Plan B for our stressful lives. Or we need to decide how much we can contribute financially to help our aging parents. The list can go on and on.

Being clear on what the key decisions are that you need to make in the next twelve to eighteen months will help to ensure that you both have it on the top of your minds and thus will meaningfully engage in contributing to the decision-making. Doing this explicitly and with some focus, rather than through ad-hoc snippets of random conversations, improves your communication and commitment to these decisions. Note that at this stage we aren't asking you to make the decision. We're just asking you to be explicit about the decisions that need to be made in the near future so that you are both aware of them and have them on your radar. As they say, "Awareness is half the battle"!

> MAKING DECISIONS EXPLICIT IS SOMETHING PERHAPS MORE COMMONLY DONE IN BUSINESS.

Making decisions explicit is something perhaps more commonly done in business. Often as part of the annual review and planning process, the key decisions facing the business will be articulated, giving the various stakeholders a chance to provide input into what information will be required to make the decision. We have found that couples that have significantly different views on their upcoming decisions find this to be a powerful alignment, clarification, and prioritization exercise. For those that hold similar views on the key decisions it is confirmation of the key choices ahead, a chance to consider these explicitly, and perhaps a reminder to take the time to make the choices ahead, rather than having them "shelved" while life's busy status quo continues on.

Defining your Decision Radar will also give you both a chance to "pre-think" together what information you'll need to make the decisions and will ensure that you are both bought into the need to make the decision as well as the approximate timing. This next section will give you a chance to work together on developing your own Decision Radar.

STEP 1:
Create your joint long list of upcoming decisions

Step 1 is to do a "brain dump" of the various decisions that you will need to make over the next twelve to eighteen months and document them on a single piece of paper. Set aside fifteen minutes to focus on this together. See how far you get, and if you need a bit more time, then give yourself another fifteen minutes to identify them. You should be able to get to a good first draft within this time. Remember, you aren't trying to solve the problem or make the decision now; you're just documenting decisions that you will need to make in the near future. After you complete your first draft of your Decision Radar, you may have additional decisions come to mind which you can add to your list and iterate the document as a second revision.

These decisions could include anything from deciding what color to paint the kitchen, to whether to proceed with optional surgery, to when to purchase a new car. It might include which daycare to send your child to and how much money to contribute to your ailing parents to improve their quality of life. Or whether to take your first skiing holiday this year to introduce the kids to the sport. Basically as many decisions that you can each think of that need to be made in the near term that are each swimming around in your minds, but that have not yet all been documented all together. It's important that you ensure that you've both contributed to this list, as you will place different relative importance on different areas. A bullet point list at this stage is fine. This is your Decision Radar - the long list version.

Step 2:
Prioritizing Your Decision Radar

From your long list, the next step is to prioritize these decisions. We suggest prioritizing based on importance and urgency. Take the time for each of you to select your top five decisions. At this stage, do this as an individual exercise, so that each of your relative prioritizations is made explicit. Try to ensure that you are capturing important and not just urgent items. Take the time for each of you to document (placing colored dots beside each of your "votes" or numbering each of your top picks) your Top 5 decisions. This will then help you to have a conversation about why you feel each is important and perhaps some of the differences that you might have in relative prioritization. Having good conversations and listening to your partners' views on why a decision seemed important to them is an important step in getting to a set of decisions that you can both commit to as being important to make.

The next step then is to create your prioritized joint list that you both believe reflects your key upcoming decisions. If you have more than 5 on your joint list, that is fine, though you may want to recognize that you may not be able to address them all at once, and may need to phase them over time.

You have now completed your Decision Radar and should now have a common view of the key planned decisions that are on the horizon for both you and your family. There may very well be new decisions that pop-up that you will be required to make. Your Decision Radar is a framework to align on your key planned decisions, but do recognize that life is dynamic and that change is a part of life. Hopefully the process of aligning your decision expectations will provide a solid base plan and an approach that will help you to address planned as well as unplanned decisions that will come up. Next we will look at Decision Roles and how to clarify the respective roles that each of you may play in a particular decision.

WHO MAKES OR IS INVOLVED IN THE DECISION?

Once you have a clear view of your Decision Radar and the key decisions that need to be made in your family, the next thing we will look at is the various Decision Roles and who is going be involved in which roles.

For complex matrix organizations, this clarity is very important and can help to address some of the politics and power struggles that can get in the way of good decision-making. Take for example a country manager in the UK, and a product manager who is responsible for selling widgets globally. Who gets to make the decision on what price to sell the widgets at in the UK? Or who decides what the next upgrade should be for the widgets in the UK? Without clear decision roles, both the country manager and the product manager might feel that they have the right to make these decisions. Being clear on where the decision lies and the role that the other manager might play will be important in maintaining good working relations and ensuring robust decision-making.

Defining decision roles within an explicit framework is something that helps to clarify some of these ambiguities and also to empower and make individuals accountable to their decisions. It also recognizes that there are different roles in making decisions – not only is there the final decision maker, but also individuals who should provide input into the decision or those who might be responsible for executing the decision, for example.

Taking into consideration decision frameworks used within leading organizations, as well as the unique needs of decisions at home, we have developed the RIDDE^{TM} framework for decision-making at home. This identifies 4 key roles within decision-making at home that we will elaborate on: Recommend, Input, Decide, and Execute.

R	Recommend:	Who is going to make an initial recommendation for the decision?
I	Input:	Who else needs to input into the decision?

DD	Decide:	Who will make the final decision? Consider whether it should be a joint decision (and hence 2D's or "DD") or one made solo?
E	Execute:	Who will ensure the decision is executed and action is taken?

Recommend (R):

This is the person who will do the groundwork to frame, coordinate and recommend a decision from some explicit alternatives. Take for example the purchase of a new car - this person would do the research, understand the requirements of stakeholders, narrow down the alternatives, and make a recommendation.

Input (I):

This person (or people) have the right to input into the decision, and have to the right to be listened to, but don't make the final decision. So, for example, they may want to state a preference for color or size or whether the car is automatic or manual. They may also want to input a price range.

Decide (DD):

This is the person (or people) responsible for the decision. Typically, in the business context, there is a single decision maker. This helps to ensure single point accountability and clarity for the organization. However, at home, we feel that there are many decisions that actually need to be joint decisions, hence the "DD." There are as well decisions that one or the other partner will make as a sole decision maker - so sometimes it will be single "D" (Decide) and other times double "DD" (joint decision). The decision maker(s) has/have the final call on the decision at hand.

It is important that you are clear on who this is as there will, inevitably, be times when things don't go exactly as they should, but if there is buy-in that the approach and process was correct, then it is easier to stick together through the consequences and perhaps any resultant actions rather than placing blame or pointing fingers at each other.

In the example of the purchase of a car, perhaps both partners need to actually agree to the final decision on which car they purchase – especially if it is a car that will have shared usage. Or perhaps there is one partner who is more particular about the vehicle choice and the other is quite relaxed and agrees that they don't need or even want to have the final say. Or if it is a second vehicle, perhaps the primary driver will have the sole final decision right on it, while the other will provide input only.

Execute (E):

The person who executes is the one responsible for making sure that the decision actually gets implemented. Many times decisions are made, but then it is assumed that the other person will actually follow through with things, or it has been left ambiguous and so nothing ends up being done. As time goes by, nothing actually changes despite the decision nominally being made.

In the case of the car, this might involve all the test drives, arranging financing, insurance, any vehicle taxes, etc. Basically, this includes all the implementation activities that need to happen before you can actually be off and driving in the new vehicle. One of you may be better suited to the tasks of implementation. Or one of you may have more interest and expertise in the area or more available time to actually follow-up on all the tasks. How you choose to identify who will execute the actions may vary depending on the decision at hand, however recognizing that you should have a common understanding of who will be executing the decision will help to avoid misunderstandings and ensure that your decisions do, in fact, get implemented as smoothly as possible!

Let's look at two scenarios related to the car purchase example. In Scenario 1, a couple are looking to purchase their first car which will have shared usage. In this case, the wife works part-time and has more time to do the "leg-work" of recommending a few options which she feels meet their requirements. They have decided that they both need to input into the decision – although they may value different attributes. For example, the wife may have a strong point of view on car size, reliability of the brand and price, while the husband may be more concerned about the color and how it drives.

Together, they both have input into the requirements of their vehicle. In this case, they have agreed that they both need to agree on the final car purchase and thus are both decision-makers (DD). They agree that the wife will follow-up with all the executional items, given her greater time flexibility.

In Scenario 2, we look at a decision to purchase a secondary car for the wife who will be the primary driver. Perhaps the rationale for who makes the recommendation and who needs to input are similar to Scenario 1. Although in this case, perhaps the husband would have less or different input requirements (price and safety, for example). But in this case, they decide that the decision-maker will be solely the wife, as she is the primary driver. Given the different nature of the decision, Scenario 2 merited different decision roles from Scenario 1.

RIDDE™ Decision framework – Car purchase example		
	Scenario 1 – Shared vehicle	Scenario 2 – Secondary vehicle for wife
R - Recommend	Wife	Wife
I – Input	Husband & Wife	Husband & Wife
DD - Decide	Husband & Wife	Wife
E - Execute	Wife	Wife

Let's look at another example. This time the decision is whether to have your ailing mother-in-law come to live with you. If it is the husband's mother, the decision roles might be as follows:

RIDDE™ Decision framework	
	Mother in Law moving in example
R - Recommend	Husband
I – Input	Husband, Wife, Mother, Husband's siblings, Mother's doctor, children
DD - Decide	Husband & Wife
E - Execute	Husband

The RIDDE™ framework provides a common language and approach for couples and their families to talk through the process of how decisions, especially big ones, will be approached before actually trying to make these decisions. Ensuring that you both agree on who will be involved in which decisions will help to avoid some of the decision "pitfalls" and potential misunderstandings that might otherwise be avoided. Over time, you will fine-tune your approach to applying this framework. Often it is enough to have the common language to ask the questions "Is this a joint decision?" or "Do you want me to take the lead on execution?" or even to have the permission to make assertions "I'd like to input into that decision". While there may be other key decisions where you want spend more time talking through involvement in each decision role in more detail. We have found that this framework allows couples to decipher where and how they can improve on their decisions while still choosing how rigorously to apply it. The spirit is not to turn every decision into an overburdened process, but to both be aware of the different roles in decisions so that you can apply them with the tailored rigor or "light touch" that the particular decision merits.

How do we define our Decision Roles?

You can start to work through your Decision Roles by building on your previously agreed Decision Radar. Use the RIDDE™ framework to identify who needs to be involved in which decisions.

STEP 1:
Evaluate a past decision process

Choose a recent decision that you have made and evaluate your respective roles through the RIDDE™ framework. This might be anything from deciding to host an 80th birthday celebration for your mum, to deciding whether to adjust your investment portfolio, to deciding how long your in-laws should visit for or where to go for your next family holiday. Identify who implicitly took on each of the 4 roles : Recommend, Input, Decide, and Execute.

R	Recommend:	Who is going to make an initial recommendation for the decision?
I	Input:	Who else needs to input into the decision?
DD	Decide:	Who will make the final decision? Consider whether it should be a joint decision (and hence 2D's or "DD") or one made solo?
E	Execute:	Who will ensure the decision is executed and action is taken?

How well did the roles you each took for this particular decision work in each of your opinions? What worked well and not so well?

Now that you've had a chance to reflect on a past decision, you might want to review a few more. Sometimes patterns emerge that are helpful to identify. Often reviewing some decisions that worked well as well as some that didn't go so well in one or other of your opinions is helpful.

The purpose of Step 1 is to give you a chance to reflect how you are currently making decisions and who is tending to be involved in which areas of decision-making. Perhaps one of you is a "control freak" and getting involved in all the nuances of every decision. This might frustrate your partner or disempower them. Or perhaps one of you is making the decisions, but then never following up on execution and actions - so it's all talk and no action. Or maybe the other partner is left with all the execution, adding to their workload and perhaps to some resentment. Take the time to conclude what your current pattern of behavior is related to decision roles, and perhaps what might be a more ideal way to make your decisions going forwards. You can move on to Step 2 when you are ready.

STEP 2:
Evaluate future decision roles

Select one of the decisions from the Decision Radar that you created earlier in this chapter. Apply the RIDDE^{TM} framework to this upcoming decision identifying who will Recommend, Input, Decide and Execute the decision. You can reflect on your observations from Step 1 from your past decision-making as well as what you think will work best for the specific decision at hand.

As you work your way through this example, make sure that both of you have enough "airtime" to voice your thoughts on who should be involved when. You may want to consider how you have operated in the past and go along with similar roles or perhaps try a new approach. You may want to play to your strengths, so if one of you is particularly knowledgeable or interested in a certain area, like finances, you may want to be the one recommending these decisions. The key benefit is to have a framework and common language for communicating how you jointly want to approach decisions.

Not all decisions will be proven right over time, but it's important to have agreed on how the decision was made and the role that you each played. This appreciation and respect for each other's involvement will help lead to a positive outcome and enable you to work together on improving future decisions together.

Congratulations on completing Life Management Strategy 5 - agreeing on the "what" and "who" of decisions. You have now completed all five of the Life Management Strategies. We hope that through the process you have had robust and meaningful conversations and have a common language and more complete "tool-kit" for working together on strategic and operational planning and key decision-making at home.

Chapter Eight Notes:
STRATEGY 5: AGREE THE "WHAT" AND "WHO" OF DECISIONS

Our **thoughts** and **next steps** from completing:

- Our Decision Radar
- Our Decision Roles

Thoughts:

_____
_____
_____
_____
_____
_____
_____
_____
_____
_____

Next Steps:

Chapter Nine

CREATING THE VIRTUOUS CYCLE

Now that you have completed the 5 Life Management Strategies, you can start applying them regularly to become part of a virtuous cycle at home. What do we mean by a virtuous cycle? Well, something that you will reap increasing rewards from over time - the more you work at it, the better it will get. As you continue to apply the frameworks, they will start to become second nature and you will also find how to tailor them to best suit your needs. You might even think of other frameworks that you use in your work world that you'd like to start applying to your home life. Most of all, we hope that this will help you to communicate and work together better and thus continue to grow together over time.

How often?

How often you choose to review and redraft your 5 Life Management Strategies is something that will depend on how much change you have in your life, and it also differs by strategy. Here is some guidance:

Strategy 1 - Define Your Home Culture (Vision, Mission and Values)

Culture is something that, once you have defined it and are happy with it, you shouldn't need to make radical changes to regularly. We review this annually, but typically it doesn't change much.

Strategy 2 - Agree Your 5-Year Strategic Plan

You will want to review your 5-Year Strategic Plan annually. Not the least because you'll want to extend it out a further year, to reflect the year that has passed. Typically about 80% of it will stay the same, but you will want to reflect on the year past and the impact on the next five years. There may at times be a point of inflection in your life - perhaps job loss or relocation or a death or birth - that may merit a fresh look at your five-year plan. In this case, you may want to refresh and redraft your plan to reflect the current state of your life, but still taking into consideration the goals you had previously made and deciding whether to stay or move away from them given the new context.

Strategy 3 - Memorize Your 3-5 Key Annual Priorities

Annual priorities will change by definition each year when you select the ones most relevant for the year ahead. We also suggest that you revisit these in year bi- annually or quarterly reviews to ensure they continue to reflect the priorities for the current year. You'll also want to ensure that your behaviors and resource allocation (especially your time and energy) are reflecting the choices you have made.

Strategy 4 - Detail Your Annual Operating Plan

Your Annual Operating Plan should be a "living" plan." You should try to review it in some form or other quarterly (four times per year) to keep track of what has been done and perhaps to review new activities that have come up. Having this conversation quarterly helps to keep you on track and communicating about what and why certain activities are your priorities. It allows you to reflect your dynamic life at the planning stage, smoothing the execution that follows. We like to do this over a dinner out – good food and good conversation!

STRATEGY 5 - AGREE THE "WHAT" AND "WHO" OF DECISIONS

Creating your Decision Radar is good to do annually. You can revisit these perhaps bi- annually or quarterly to add any new key decisions to your Decision Radar and reflect on the ones that you have made to date.

Your Decision Roles framework is one that is good to embed in your behaviors of how you make decisions. It may be as simple as saying "Who's going to make the decision on this one?" or "Do you want to input into this decision?" Acknowledging and clarifying your respective roles in upcoming decisions can go a long way. When you have a particularly difficult decision, you may want to formally use the framework and agree on all the roles. Or if you are particularly unhappy or believe that your decision-making processes are "broken," then we would suggest using the framework explicitly until you are back on the right track.

We try to start our annual planning process around October of the prior calendar year. That way we've reviewed all 5 Life Management Strategies by about November so that we can enter the next calendar year aligned on our direction and priorities. We save these Annual plan "packs" and place our latest family photo along with the year on the cover. It helps us to feel that

> EVERY FAMILY ENDS UP SOMEWHERE, BUT FEW FAMILIES END UP SOMEWHERE ON PURPOSE.

we have placed appropriate value and tailored it to be "our" unique family plan. It is a document that charts our aspirations, our celebrations, and our journey as a family together. It is also always nice to review the past year and to recognize what we have accomplished together. We hope that you also will find these 5 Life Management Strategies as valuable as we and others have. Every family ends up somewhere, but few families end up somewhere on purpose.

We wish you a wonderful journey together as you Work Together and Grow Together as a couple and a family!

ABOUT THE AUTHORS

LISA HAS A B. Sc. Engineering from Queen's University in Canada and a MBA from INSEAD in France and Singapore and has worked at leading international companies including Procter & Gamble and Monitor strategy consulting.

MARIO HAS A Bachelor of Environmental Studies from University of Waterloo in Canada and a M.Sc. from University of Leeds in the UK and is a Director at IBI Group.

Together, they have over 40 years experience in the corporate world internationally building and leading great teams. They started applying business frameworks to their home life early on in their marriage and it has become a key part of happily managing life at home, strategically and operationally. They are Co-Founders of The Marriage Development Company and live with their family in London, England.

TO FIND OUT MORE VISIT:

www.SmartBusinessThinkingAtHome.com

www.ingramcontent.com/pod-product-compliance
Lightning Source LLC
Chambersburg PA
CBHW080415170426
43194CB00015B/2819